UNCOMMON

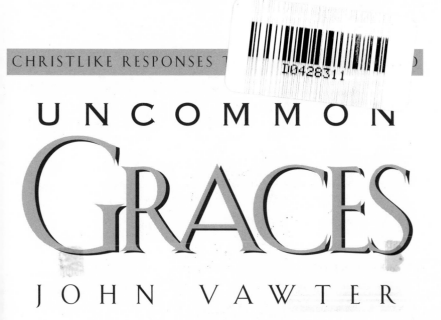

GRACES

JOHN VAWTER

DISCARD

NAVPRESS

BRINGING TRUTH TO LIFE

NavPress Publishing Group

P.O. Box 35001, Colorado Springs, Colorado 80935

The Navigators is an international Christian organization. Our mission is to reach, disciple, and equip people to know Christ and to make Him known through successive generations. We envision multitudes of diverse people in the United States and every other nation who have a passionate love for Christ, live a lifestyle of sharing Christ's love, and multiply spiritual laborers among those without Christ.

NavPress is the publishing ministry of The Navigators. NavPress publications help believers learn biblical truth and apply what they learn to their lives and ministries. Our mission is to stimulate spiritual formation among our readers.

© 1998 by John Vawter
All rights reserved. No part of this publication may be reproduced in any form without written permission from NavPress, P.O. Box 35001, Colorado Springs, CO 80935.

Library of Congress Catalog Card Number 98-2879

ISBN 1-57683-043-8

Cover photo by Photodisc

Some of the anecdotal illustrations in this book are true to life and are included with the permission of the persons involved. All other illustrations are composites of real situations, and any resemblance to people living or dead is coincidental.

Unless otherwise identified, all Scripture quotations in this publication are taken from the HOLY BIBLE: NEW INTERNATIONAL VERSION ® (NIV ®). Copyright © 1973, 1978, 1984 by International Bible Society. Used by permission of Zondervan Publishing House. All rights reserved. The other version used is *The New Testament in Modern English* (PH), J. B. Phillips Translator, copyright © J. B. Phillips 1958, 1960, 1972, used by permission of Macmillan Publishing Company.

Printed in the United States of America

Vawter, John.
    Uncommon graces: Christlike responses to a hostile world/John Vawter.
        p. cm.
    ISBN 1-57683-043-8 (pbk.)
    1. Virtues. 2. Christian life. I. Title.
    BV4630.V38   1998
    241'.4—dc21   98-2879
                                                                          CIP

1 2 3 4 5 6 7 8 9 10 11 12 13 14 15 / 05 04 03 02 01 00 99 98

FOR A FREE CATALOG OF
NAVPRESS BOOKS & BIBLE STUDIES,
CALL 1-800-366-7788 (USA)
or 1-416-499-4615 (CANADA)

*This book is dedicated to my wonderful
daughter, Stephanie,
and to my two colleagues at the
Murdock Charitable Trust
who challenged me to write it,
Dr. Steve Nicholson and John Woodyard.*

CONTENTS

Foreword

As a boy not yet old enough to drive, I spent a lot of time in the car with my mother behind the wheel. Whenever another driver extended special courtesy, she always said, "He must be a Christian." In my youthful naiveté I developed a simplistic but delightful worldview in which acts of courtesy and kindness proved a person's relationship with Jesus Christ and acts of discourtesy and unkindness proved a person to be an unbeliever.

As an adult I realize it's not always that simple. I now know that unbelievers sometimes behave graciously and Christians sometimes honk their horns, drive selfishly, and display obscene gestures. But, I still choose to believe that those whose lives are committed to Jesus Christ are the ones most likely to demonstrate such uncommon graces of gentleness, attentiveness, loyalty, candor, mercy, kindness, and others.

My own experiences have been largely positive. I have seen men and women act Christianly in the worst of circumstances. I have been blessed by the amazing forgiveness, generosity, tolerance, and love of those whom I have offended. I have been impressed, shaped, and molded by the real life godliness of ordinary Christians. It is a wonder to behold. And, having experienced such powerful Christian good, I yearn for more and more. Just imagine if every follower of Jesus Christ not only received grace from God but consistently gave grace to others!

Of course, the number one reason for Christians to live Christianly is Christ. Our motivation to do good is to please Jesus and be like Jesus. But there is a second powerful motivation—seeing the impact of our grace in the lives of others.

Victor Hugo's classic *Les Misérables* keeps coming back to the public in stage musicals and screen movies. It is the story of a convict who is treated kindly by a French bishop who gives him a place to stay in the bishop's home. In return for generous hospitality, the convict steals the bishop's silver. He is arrested by the police who have the man, the stolen goods, and every intent of sending him back to prison and hard labor. However, the bishop insists that the silver is a gift and the man is set free. The impact of the bishop's uncommon grace is so profound that the convict's life is transformed. Unexpected love, forgiveness, and generosity change him from a hardened criminal into a respectable civil leader whose entire life is marked by kindness to others. He, too, becomes a man of uncommon graces.

Imagine if we were all like that bishop, returning good for evil, love for hate, generosity for greed, and hope for hopelessness. We would be more than like the bishop; we would be just like Jesus!

John Vawter has candidly and compassionately tackled the topic and the tension. He is no do-good wimp who blindly allows others to take unfair advantage of him. He is no hardened legalist who knows the law but forgets the grace. John realistically understands our complex human nature and calls us to live uncommonly and graciously as Christians who represent Jesus and transform others.

DR. LEITH ANDERSON

ACKNOWLEDGMENTS

THERE ARE A NUMBER OF PEOPLE WHOM I WISH TO RECOGNIZE for their help on this project:

Dr. Robert and Cheryl Moeller, who kept saying, "There is a book in there somewhere," and who helped me take the first steps.

Bruce and Becky Duross Fish, who did the editing and offered their encouragement.

Dr. Ray Burwick, Dr. David Fisher, Nona Hovey, Reuel Nygaard, Cecil Schmidt, and Dr. Jim Wetherbe, all of whom either read or kept encouraging me that I could finish the project.

June Simons, my English composition instructor at the University of Oregon in 1962, who challenged me constantly to work harder in her classes. Professor Simons, wherever you are, I have not forgotten you or your positive challenges to me.

John Michael Vawter, my terrific son, whose pride in "Pop" writing a book both encouraged and thrilled me.

Ken Gire, for his gentle but firm guidance and his editing skills as we worked together through the last editing stages. Ken is a gentleman and a fine Christian, and it has been my privilege to work with him. He has touched my life.

The gracious people who allowed me to use their stories.

And finally, I wish to thank my wonderful wife, Susan, who encouraged me and kept me looking forward when the words did not seem to come.

INTRODUCTION

WE LIVE IN A WORLD WHERE SHOWING GRACE IS UNCOMMON.

The very idea of grace seems weak in a world that is aggressive, competitive, and often violent. You hear something of the world's violence every day. Not long ago, I was driving through a major southwestern city, and over the radio I heard a warning from the police urging motorists to avoid violent confrontations after traffic accidents. Just that day, a driver had been shot and killed by another motorist after a minor mishap. Less serious, but still troubling, are the signs that appear in some businesses. I still have vivid memories of a sign in a souvenir shop that read, "Shoplifters will be beaten to death," and of a slogan aimed at children by a major taco franchise, "Shut up and eat your beans."

Sadly, we find ourselves living in a world that is ruder and cruder than any of us wants. Perhaps that accounts for the unraveling of the social fabric around us and the need to replace manners with laws. Consequently, as Jerald Jellison writes, "The question, 'Is it proper?' has been replaced by the question, 'Is it legal?'"[1] Martin Smith, a syndicated columnist, speaks for many of us when he asks, "What social pathology explains the reluctance of so many people to pull over for passing funeral processions, to make small talk with fellow bus passengers, to exchange the pleasantries that for generations helped lubricate social discourse?"[2]

Some say it is because we live in a graceless era. Others say it is because we are all in a fight for survival in which diminishing resources and rising expectations make us more aggressive. Regardless of the cause, it's clear these problems are pervasive.

> Lamentations about the decline of common courtesy and civility transcend economic, social and racial lines, says Smith. Experts agree on the symptoms but aren't sure how to explain the decline of civility and the rise of crudeness. They cite everything from the anti-Establishment movement of the 1960s to the unraveling of close-knit neighborhoods to the rise of feminism.[3]

As evidence of the declining state of common graces, Smith points to the World Cup Soccer Championship that was held in the United States. He was amazed as competitors from other nations frequently helped each other up from the field, winners consoling losers, teams treating one another with dignity. "The behavior was very different from the in-your-face style of more traditional U.S. sports."[4]

I wish I could say things were different in the church. Unfortunately, many of the unkind, demeaning, and dehumanizing trends at work in our culture have found their way into the church. Here are just a few examples: An angry parishioner drives his car all over the pastor's lawn to express frustration over something that is said in church. The leader of a large Christian ministry demands unconditional support from his employees, and if they fail to live up to his demands, he threatens to "cut their tails off." The list of examples, tragically, could go on and on.

The late Francis Schaeffer was right when he observed that the spirit of the age always finds its way into the church. Far too often, we who claim to follow Christ have learned to tolerate careless words, rude behavior, and sinful practices.

Fortunately for all of us, the grace of God remains visible in the life of Jesus. Its bright and steady beacon searches our lives and shines throughout the world. It was the light of divine grace that led us to Him in the first place, and through us it can lead others to Him. But the purity, beauty, and intensity of that light can be diminished in a number of ways. Practicing the uncommon graces of Christ's life is what keeps the light shining—and what gives hope to a world of lengthening shadows.

The light radiates from the inside of us out. And it is there, on the inside, where the power of the Holy Spirit combines with a few personal disciplines to light the lamp. To keep it lit takes diligence. We need to begin each day with a serious moral inventory to see if we are living up to our Lord's example. We also need to seek the intervention of the Holy Spirit to control our reactions to the normal provocations of life in a fallen world. Such moral and spiritual disciplines keep the wick trimmed in our own lives and in our relationships with others.

I hope this book helps in some way toward that end. When I started writing it, the words of Ciclia de Baca caught my eye. He said, "I keep wanting to do a remember-when book. Remember when someone sneezed and everyone would say, 'God bless you'? Remember when people would see an older person and offer them their seat?"[5] Well, *Uncommon Graces* is not that book. Rather than a "remember-when" book, it's a "why-not-today?" book.

Why can't you and I make a difference in our world by practicing the simple courtesies of grace? And why can't we begin making that difference today?

To begin, we must start where God started.

With Jesus.

PART ONE

THE
UNCOMMON
GRACES

CHAPTER 1

GENTLENESS

SOMEONE ONCE TOLD ME OF HIS EXPERIENCE WITH A professor that illustrates the power of gentleness: "During my last term of seminary, I was looking forward to sitting under a professor renowned for his scholarship and keen mind. But when I finally got a seat in his class, I was stunned.

"The professor walked up and down the classroom aisles, stopping in front of a student's desk and firing off a semi-automatic round of questions. The barrage continued until the student was caught in a contradiction. Here's a sampling of the interrogations:

'Mr. Smith, have you ever committed adultery?'

'No,' the student said.

'Mr. Smith, do you believe in the Bible?'

'Yes.'

'Do you believe in it wholeheartedly?'

'Yes.'

'Would you ever disobey it?'

'Not knowingly.'

'Do you believe that Jesus always spoke the truth?'

'Yes.'

'Do you believe that Jesus spoke the truth when He said that if a man looks on a woman with lust in his heart, he has already committed adultery?'

'Yes.'

'Have you ever looked on a woman with lust?'

'Yes, I guess so.'

'Then, Mr. Smith, you have committed adultery. You lied.'

"I grew increasingly uncomfortable with how the professor treated us. It didn't seem possible that Jesus would treat anyone this way. And it didn't seem right to just sit back and let him abuse us. I wanted to talk to him in private, but this professor was a thoroughly intimidating man. *What if he got angry and chewed me out? What if he lowered my grade for daring to challenge his authority?*

"In the end, I decided to go to his office outside of normal student conference hours. I remember approaching his door with a prayer that God would help me maintain a gentle spirit. I planned to ask for only a few minutes of his time and wanted to avoid any hint of rudeness. Above all, I wanted to respect his position of authority.

'Professor, may I have five minutes with you?'

'Yes. Please come in.'

'Professor, I'd like to ask you just one question.'

'Yes?'

'Would you be willing to pray and ask God if He approves of how you treat the students in your class?'

'What?'

"A look of surprise and irritation crossed his face.

"I repeated the question, trying to hide the tremble in my voice.

"The professor bristled and leaned forward. 'Young man, you don't have a scheduled appointment with me right now, do you?'

" 'No,' I said, 'but I asked you for five minutes, and you said I could have them.' I glanced down at my watch. 'I've only taken three, so I have two minutes left. I'm not asking you to respond to me. I just ask you to ask God privately if He approves of how you treat the students in your class.'

"His only response was a long, cold gaze.

"I stood up and extended my hand. The professor reluctantly shook it.

"'Thanks for your time,' I said, then left the office.

"While I never got a direct response from him, the heat-lamp interrogations disappeared, at least in *that* class.'"

The student succeeded because he followed Solomon's wisdom in Proverbs 25:15: "Through patience a ruler can be persuaded, and a gentle tongue can break a bone." He succeeded because he was gentle. He didn't challenge the power the professor was wielding with a greater power of his own. The student approached the professor in a respectful manner to uncover an area of his life where change was needed, but he left the final persuading up to God. If we want to demonstrate the uncommon grace of Jesus to a world that worships power, we must set aside our combativeness to embrace gentleness.

A SOCIETY THAT'S "IN-YOUR-FACE"

Embracing gentleness isn't easy because we live in a world where gentleness is a rare commodity—even in someplace as middle America as Minnesota.

When I lived there, the police chief of Minneapolis came under fire from the city council, the mayor, and the police union. He fought hard to keep his job but ultimately was pushed out. The whole process of his removal was anything but gentle. At his final press conference he said, "I do not mind tough questions, I do not mind tough issues, but please, treat me like an equal, another human being. . . . I deserve that. Everybody deserves that. When that doesn't happen, it's intolerable, inexcusable."[1]

Others, like Alexander Moore, echo the police chief's concern about harsh and irrational treatment. Moore, who is an anthropology professor at the University of Southern California, observes rampant rudeness at work everywhere in our society. He feels it grew out of the confrontational spirit of the Sixties.[2] Activists used boycotts, sit-ins, protest marches, and threats to achieve their goals. Over the last thirty years, we have learned to view such activities as routine. Today confrontation is one part of a destructive code of conduct that enflames our relationships with one another. When violent confrontation is a normal part of our lives, there's little room left for gentleness.

The rise in negative political ads during the last decade is another indicator that "in-your-face" confrontation has become an accepted part of American life.

Most of us remember the Willie Horton ad that helped George Bush beat Michael Dukakis by portraying the governor as irresponsible in his treatment of convicted criminals. The ad was widely criticized as both racist and inaccurate. Still, it contributed to a Bush victory by sowing seeds of doubt about our personal safety under a Dukakis presidency.

Bill Clinton was equally successful in portraying all Republicans as "welfare slashers" in the 1996 election. The truth was that both Democrats and Republicans were looking for ways to limit the growth of all entitlement programs because they made up such a large part of the federal budget. These ads are created only to help win elections. They work because many of us are moved by the confrontational spirit they project and the simplistic stereotyping they contain.

The media also has picked up on the appeal of this "in-your-face" philosophy. CNN's *Crossfire* and ABC's *Politically Incorrect* routinely feature individuals who interrupt, insult, and generally mistreat one another. These programs pile up impressive ratings, but they take the dignity of public debate down several notches. They encourage the dangerous notion that anyone who disagrees with us is our enemy and should be destroyed by any means necessary.

It wasn't always this way.

One of my early recollections of a political campaign dates back to 1972. George McGovern and Hubert Humphrey were vying for the Democratic nomination for president. The microphones were on when the two met on stage for a debate. The exchange before the debate went something like this:

"Good to see you, Hubert."

"Nice to see you, George."

"How's Muriel?"

"Good. How's Eleanor?"

Then for the next hour they vigorously and sometimes heatedly debated the issues. When the official exchange ended, the two men again shook hands.

"See you soon, George. Greet Eleanor for me."

"Thanks. Hello to Muriel."

It was clear that these two men had great personal respect for each other. They were attacking each other politically, not personally. It was a debate about principles, not personalities.

The Church Becomes Hostile Territory

Since the era of Vietnam, Watergate, and other national scandals, a confrontational spirit also has crept into the church. The Sixties legacy of violent protest has combined with a growing distrust of authority figures to make our churches hostile territory, especially for pastors and other church leaders. Even ordinary church members often are caught up in power struggles and various kinds of conflict. I've seen more than I care to remember. Unfortunately, some I can't help but remember.

One I vividly recall took place in a church I once pastored, where a member criticized me relentlessly. I met with the man privately and said, "Please, Adam, I don't want to play war games with you. I want to be your pastor. I want to grow with you. I want to be your friend."

Adam shrugged his shoulders, said little, and walked away.

Some time later, I was playing golf with a friend of his. "You know, Adam is always asking me about your family, your relationship with your kids, and your personal life," said the man. "I think he's trying to find areas of weakness in your life."

"Why would he do that?"

"I guess his own father was a pastor and was never home," the man replied.

"Oh, now I get it. He's still angry with his father. He's projecting that anger toward me. He's assuming I must have the same type of poor relationship with my kids that his own dad had with him."

Because we live in a culture that teaches us to distrust authority and to confront anyone we dislike, it's gotten easier for Christians to mistreat one another. We're surrounded with "in-your-face" thinking, and that influence follows us through the church doors.

In such a society, those of us who have committed ourselves to Jesus Christ as Savior and Lord must make certain we are being channels for His grace and love. If grace has become a rare commodity in our day, perhaps it is because we have forgotten Paul's warning in Romans 12:2: "Don't let the world around you squeeze you into its own mould, but let God re-make you so that your whole attitude of mind is changed. Thus you will prove in practice that the will of God's good, acceptable to him and perfect"(PH).

An Endless Search For Enemies

In the church, as in society, our confrontational approach is not limited to how we treat those in authority. A more troubling attitude is also at work. It says, "If you don't agree with me, you're my enemy."

As Christians, one way we do this is by putting our general preferences, our personal convictions, and our most important doctrinal positions on an equal level. As a result, if someone doesn't see eye to eye with us on every single cultural, economic, political, moral, and theological issue, we think we have the right to be belligerent toward them.

This problem became painfully clear to me when I heard of a conversation a friend had at the time President Clinton's mother died. My friend doesn't agree with every decision that President Clinton has made, but when the President's mother passed away, this man felt genuine sympathy for him. Not only did the President have to deal with a very difficult loss, but just as soon as he had buried his mother, he had to board a plane for an important meeting with the Russians. My friend tried to explain to a Christian acquaintance how he was feeling: "I know that when I buried my father, it took a toll on me. I was ineffective for a long while afterward."

The other man's first response was, "Did you know his mother went to the horse track?"

My friend was stunned. As he listened to his acquaintance ramble on, he soon realized that this other man hated Bill Clinton. Because he disagreed with the President's politics, it made Clinton his enemy. That meant that anyone associated with the President also had to be his enemy. His obsessive hatred had caused him to dehumanize the President's mother. Her presence at the racetrack was an excuse to keep him from feeling any sort of compassion toward her or the President. It was just one more reason to hate Bill Clinton.

I've known far too many Christians who are like this. Their lives seethe with anger, which they try to explain away as conviction. After years of seeing this kind of thing happen in churches, I've come to a surprising conclusion: Anger is not the root problem—dishonesty is.

THE HIDDEN CULT OF DISHONESTY

Dr. Ray Burwick is a professional counselor in Birmingham, and I once heard him make a remarkable statement. "Some of the smartest people who come to see me are the best liars. They pay money to sit there for sixty minutes and lie."

"Why would they do that?" I asked.

"Because they don't want to face their own weaknesses," he said.

His comments really struck home. I know this happens more often in my life than I would like to admit, and it's likely that you struggle with it as well. When we fail to confront our weaknesses honestly and regularly, we end up deceiving ourselves and those around us.

This deception is subtle because it often grows out of deep and very personal hurts we have suffered but are unwilling to face. To make ourselves feel better, we criticize something else—or some*one* else. In the process, we become secret members of a hidden cult of dishonesty within the church.

Liars for Christ.

Dishonesty makes the church a dangerous place, full of dark and deceptive shadows. Rather than learning the hard discipline of speaking the truth in love, we learn instead to cover up our resentments. We think the cover-up hides the issue. But resentments have an artesian quality about them, and they're always bubbling up somewhere else: A bit of gossip over the phone. A sarcastic comment over lunch. A refusal to return a phone call. An outburst at a committee meeting. In the process, gentleness is driven out the door, and some truly bizarre situations slip in to fill the vacancy.

I once heard about a denominational state committee that wanted to get rid of its superintendent. Committee members constantly criticized his performance behind his back, yet no one ever sat down to explain his shortcomings. The situation was made worse by the lack of any written job description for his position. Such an objective set of criteria would have forced the committee to face its dishonesty, treat the superintendent with Christian courtesy, and tell him, "You're not doing a good job. You need to improve in these areas."

Instead, for five years in a row, they refused to give him a raise. Eventually, he got the message and left. The committee members felt justified in their actions. According to their standards, they had done nothing wrong. No one expressed disapproval of the superintendent, and no one said anything ugly about him—at least, not to his face. No one shouted at him, and no one cursed him. In their eyes, the man was handled in a very Christian way.

I wonder how it looked in God's eyes. I wonder how He felt about that half decade of their punishing, demeaning, and humiliating this man, not simply by refusing to give him a raise but by refusing to grant him the dignity of an honest discussion about their concerns.

I can't say what God saw through His eyes, but I can say what I saw through mine. There was nothing Christian about what they did. There was no grace and there was no truth in how they treated him. From what I saw, they were liars—lying to the superintendent, lying to themselves, and lying to God.

Compare the dishonesty of that situation with the honesty of this one. In a doctoral class that I was teaching at one of the leading seminaries in the country, one pastor wrote this:

> Hello, my name is Ron, and I am a liar. Oh, I don't tell big black lies—just little white ones. In fact, some may not call them lies at all. They might say I have good intentions but don't always follow through with them. If you were to ask my children, they'd probably just say that Dad always changes his mind. Others may say I don't keep my word. What I haven't been, to use the popular phrase, is a "promise keeper." This awakening didn't come all of a sudden. It came over a

period of time, through the process of reading books and seeing how the years had eaten away at the trust my wife and kids used to have in me. Before you wonder what kind of ogre I am, let me clarify. I am a decent dad, a kind and patient husband, and a great pastor. My wife respects me, though the "little foxes" have eaten away at the love she once felt. But I am in the process of changing. I am going to be more intentional about the commitments I make, more proactive instead of reactive, and I am going to rely on God's strength to change me.

I was shocked that he would be so honest. But then I realized that this was a person who was genuinely committed to letting Christ deal with the issues in his life, even the little white lies that seem so safe to tell.

THE FATAL ATTRACTION OF "SAFE SINS"

Dr. Dennis Baker, former General Director of the Conservative Baptist Association, says,

> Every social system breeds its own set of sins. You have to be strong to swim against the current they generate. And if you get healthy enough to recognize what is happening and refuse to go along with it anymore, the system will turn and attack you. You will be left with the choice of either leaving the group and its dysfunctional system or being victimized by it. [3]

At one time or another, we all have found ourselves involved in churches or other Christian institutions where some pattern of sin was neither acknowledged nor corrected. One way we try to survive in such an environment is to isolate ourselves from the negatives and focus on the positives.

Item received & put in transit

Transit date: 3/6/2014, 1:05:
Title: Uncommon groun... that little companies to
a host!
Item ID: 30116489/ 4
Transit to: MADISON
Transit reason: TRANSIT

The problem with this strategy is that our standing within the organization may survive, but if it does, it survives at the expense of our spiritual lives. You see, what we participate in is not the root issue. What we tolerate is. For in time, toleration leads to participation.

According to Dr. Baker, such groups often tolerate and even promote standards of behavior that have nothing to do with a healthy commitment to Jesus Christ. As long as we are a part of the Christian subculture, we will be vulnerable to such "safe sins"—sins that are tolerated, making them "safe" to commit. The problem with "safe sins" is that, in the end, they aren't. In the beginning, they nibble away at our spiritual lives, but in the end, they devour them. By tolerating these sins, we protect ourselves from the ruthless self-examination necessary to improve our lives.

When "safe sins" go unchallenged, something of a Christian fantasy religion is allowed to thrive—a religion that condemns alcohol and adultery, yet condones, say, arrogance and abrasiveness. There should be a support group in the church for those addicted to "safe sins"—an AA for the arrogant and the abrasive.

But that won't happen, because the church is obsessed with other sins. Like the church whose pastor was called on the carpet for saying he didn't believe the Bible taught total abstinence from alcohol. He came to that conclusion after a long and careful examination of both the Old and New Testaments. He wasn't trying to promote drinking. He didn't even drink himself. He was simply trying to be honest in his handling of the Scriptures. One of his most relentless critics was a man who repeatedly said, "I believe in sinless perfection, and that includes total abstinence." He accused the pastor of going soft on both personal purity and biblical theology.

As I watched this situation develop, I discovered that the man who was mercilessly berating this pastor was in his third marriage. I wondered how many times his wives had been berated like this. How many times had they been backed into a corner and beaten with his words? But such domestic disturbances were "safe sins," at least in his eyes.

No one in the congregation confronted him. No one was courageous enough to say, "Stop it. Your attack against the pastor is wrong. Your attitude is wrong. Your accusations are wrong, and we won't tolerate it."

Because they *did* tolerate it, a place was given for that man's self-deception to express itself. As a result, every antagonistic word he spoke pushed gentleness further out the door, giving room for harshness to enter the church.

TRUE GENTLENESS IS GRACIOUS AND TRUTHFUL

Such brutal behavior has become so commonplace in society and the church that we lack the clear picture of an alternative. But if there is an alternative, what does it look like? And where can we go to find it?

The Bible.

In the Bible the apostle John says, "The Word became flesh and made his dwelling among us. We have seen his glory, the glory of the One and Only, who came from the Father, *full of grace and truth*" (John 1:14, emphasis added). The Word was Jesus. When John says that Jesus was "full of grace," he was not describing someone passive or weak. Jesus was wonderfully effective in confronting people with the truth, but He did it graciously.

The story of the woman caught in adultery illustrates the balance with which Jesus exhibited these characteristics (John 8:3-11). The teachers of the Law and the Pharisees wanted to entrap Jesus, hoping to lure Him into a situation where He might contradict the Law or discredit Himself in the eyes of the people. The bait to the trap was a woman they had caught in the act of adultery. Though the Law required they also bring her partner, they failed even to mention *him*, which suggests she had been the victim of a setup.

The religious leaders wanted to put Jesus in a position where He would either have to be gentle on the criminal or gentle on the crime. Either way they had Him. In the waiting silence, the people wondered. Would Jesus stand up for the sinner . . . or for the standard? Standing up for the sinner would give evidence for the accusation that Jesus was soft on the Law, therefore an enemy of the faith. Standing up for the standard would give evidence for the accusation that He was hard on the lawbreaker, therefore an enemy of the people.

But Jesus refused to step into the steel jaws of their "either/or" trap. Instead, He turned the trap on them. "If any one of you is without sin, let him be the first to throw a stone at her." And one by one, starting with the oldest, the self-appointed jurors left. When they all were gone, Jesus asked the woman, "Has no one condemned you?" She replied, "No one, sir." And He said, "Then neither do I condemn you. Go now and leave your life of sin."

His example reminds us that we have all received grace from God and that we are all expected to pass it on. Letting the Holy Spirit develop gentleness in us is one of the ways we can do this. For me, though, it has been slow in developing, especially when I am faced with mechanical breakdowns.

I am not a mechanically talented person. When my car breaks down, I have to rely on a mechanic to tell me what needs to be done. While I was living in Minneapolis, the radio stopped working in my Volkswagen convertible. I took the car to the dealership where I had purchased it and had all the work done on it over the years. Later that afternoon I got a call from the mechanic: "Mr. Vawter, your cassette deck is broken. It will need to be replaced."

"Okay, do it," I said.

Later on that day, I picked up my car and cruised onto the highway, putting my favorite B. B. King tape into the cassette slot ("Nobody Loves Me but My Mother and She Could Be Jiving Me, Too"). Nothing happened. I wheeled the car around and headed back to the dealership.

"Excuse me, but my cassette deck still isn't working," I said to the mechanic.

"That's because the back speakers are burned out and you need to replace them, too," he replied.

I felt of tide of anger rising from my ankles and working its way up my body.

"Wait a minute. You told me the problem was the cassette deck. Shouldn't you have tested the back speakers first to make certain *they* weren't the problem?"

Another mechanic overheard our conversation and broke in, "Listen, mister, we know our business. Speakers don't burn out by themselves. The deck makes that happen."

Feeling as though they were treating me like an idiot, I instinctively wanted to strike back. But there were two of them and one of me, and I didn't need a calculator to figure the math on those odds. Besides, they were holding tools. As I paused to collect myself and consider my options, that's when things got *really* complicated. The Holy Spirit reminded me that I was a follower of Christ. What would *Jesus* do? Fight or walk away? Or would He say something that would keep Him from being forced into either of those options?

I took a deep breath. "Gentlemen, I may not be communicating well, so I apologize for that. But I'm also concerned that you're not listening to me. We need to resolve this problem."

My unexpected change of tone and attitude caught them off guard. Because I softened my approach, we were able to discuss the situation. In a few minutes, they agreed that the speakers could not have failed by themselves. In the end, they replaced the speakers free of charge. And in the process, they taught me a valuable lesson: that more can be accomplished with a few gentle words than with a toolbox full of angry ones.

TRUE GENTLENESS IS WELL-TRAINED

The apostle Paul suggested another path to gentleness when he wrote that "the fruit of the Spirit is love, joy, peace, patience, kindness, goodness, faithfulness, *gentleness* and self-control" (Galatians 5:22-23, emphasis added). The Holy Spirit works in us to create a life that is responsive to God. Gentleness is a part of that life. So is self-control. Notice how Paul ties the two together.

The word translated "gentleness" in our English Bibles can be traced back to the word for a "well-trained show horse." These animals were sturdy and strong, but their real value lay in the extensive training they received—training that made them especially responsive to their master's commands.

Our gentleness should be like those horses—well-trained.

An example of such training can be found in Matthew 26. Here we find Jesus in the Garden of Gethsemane, wrestling with the terrors of His impending crucifixion. In His agony He prays, "If it is possible, may this cup be taken from me." Then He adds, "Yet not as I will, but as you will" (Matthew 26:39).

What a remarkable scene. Jesus is at a crossroads on His way to the cross. Though the entire course of His life has led Him to this place, now that He's there He wants to turn back. Who of us wouldn't? It's an honest and very human response. He knew what was about to happen. And how much of what He knew did He already feel? The sting of the whip. The blows to the face. The pain of the nails. To say nothing of the greater pain of being separated from God.

But in the midst of it all, a lifetime of training steadied Him to stay the course to the destiny appointed by His Father. He was prepared to "[learn] obedience from what he suffered" (Hebrews 5:8). That is the path we must follow to learn gentleness. I'm not saying we should seek out suffering. I am saying, though, that if we wish to become gentle, there are things we will have to endure.

Things like humiliation.

A friend of mine is chaplain to a major college football team. During one of their games against a longtime rival, emotions were running high, and one of their star players went nuts on the field. Everyone was shocked because he was a Christian and was usually very controlled and disciplined. Yet there he was, shouting at an opposing player, even threatening him, and causing a scene in front of thousands of fans.

When the ball changed hands, he ran to the sidelines, frantically searching among teammates, asking, "Where's the chaplain? Where is he? I need to see him." When he found him, there was urgency in his eyes and his voice. "We need to pray right now. I need to get back in control of myself. I'm doing a poor job of representing Christ."

I admire that young man. Even though he was a warrior in the midst of a violent game, he understood the need to remain controlled by the Spirit of God. He was not afraid to face the truth about his behavior and humble himself in light of what he saw. This demonstrates another characteristic of true gentleness—taking responsibility for our actions.

TRUE GENTLENESS IS RESPONSIBLE

Have you noticed how many people don't assume responsibility for what they say or how they say it? Some are blind to the devastating effect they can have on others. Others can see the devastation but are unwilling to admit they have done anything wrong. When challenged, they say, "I never said that" or "I was just kidding." They're determined to save face, even if it means losing character.

I worry about falling into the same pattern myself. When my daughter Stephanie was ten or eleven, I got involved in a verbal battle with her. I walked away from it feeling a little flustered but nothing more. And I was unaware of what she felt as she walked away.

A few minutes after the confrontation, my wife, Susan, approached me. "Did you mean to leave Stephanie crying in the den?"

"She isn't crying," I said defensively.

"Yes, she is," came the gentle reply. "Go see for yourself."

I did, and she was. As I stood there, watching my daughter in tears, I knew I had to humble myself to ask her forgiveness. It was not only the responsible thing to do, it was the right thing to do.

At some time or another, we've all made someone else cry—or become frustrated—or get angry. To avoid these situations, we need an early-warning system to alert us when trouble is coming. The system I've developed is something I call the "grocery store test."

I cringe at the thought of being in a grocery store with someone I'm at odds with, where I have to duck out of sight to avoid bumping into him. When I'm wondering if a relationship is in danger, I imagine myself being in that store, with all its sights and sounds and smells. Then I imagine the other person appearing around a corner. At the moment our shopping carts collide, I ask myself, *How do I feel? What do I say?*

This exercise is a pretty accurate test of whether I've been responsible to mend the broken fences in my relationships with other people—and whether I've mended them with gentleness.

A number of years ago, I took a flight to the past, touching down for my college reunion. As I thought about the people I would be seeing, I realized there was a strained relationship with a man who lived in that city. He and I once had words over an issue involving money. While I was in town, I telephoned him and apologized for anything I had said or done to damage our relationship. He was very gracious and thanked me for my apology.

Humbling ourselves before someone we've hurt, and doing it with gentleness, is the responsible thing to do. It is also the biblical thing (Ephesians 4:1-3). And it makes going to grocery stores and class reunions a whole lot easier.

True Gentleness Is Bold

Concerned silence is another one of the "safe sins."

Let me explain what I mean by "concerned silence."

I once was hired to consult with a church that was planning to build a new auditorium. The plan already had been approved by the board and the congregation, but on the night of a leadership meeting, one man kept attacking it. His biting remarks were felt by everyone in the room. I reminded him that the congregation already had approved the project. Then he turned on me. Here was this pit bull without a muzzle, used to saying whatever he wanted, no matter how vicious. And no one restrained him. Everyone else just sat there—in concerned silence—and let him get away with it.

Afterward, I approached him and said, "Relationships are important to me. I want to make certain we're still in fellowship when I leave tonight."

"Oh, don't worry, everybody in this room understands me," he said.

"Well, I thought you were very angry and negative," I responded.

"No, I wasn't. That's just how I communicate."

"But I didn't know that. It's unfair of you to assume that everybody understands that about you. We shouldn't have to interpret your harsh words. Your speech should reflect the beauty of Christ," I said.

My purpose wasn't to reprimand the man. It was to show him compassion, caring enough about him to break the silence and challenge his behavior.

In spite of popular wisdom, silence is not *always* golden. Sometimes it is iron pyrites—fool's gold. Sometimes it deceives people, and they misinterpret our silence as approval. It takes boldness—especially in large groups—to break the silence and voice our concerns. But boldness is essential to gentleness. Without it, gentleness, like unalloyed gold, is too soft to be useful.

THE POWER OF GENTLENESS

There is often an invisible power to gentleness. See if you can notice it in the following scene between a pastor and his wife and their teenage daughter, who shocked her parents one night with the statement, "I don't believe there's a God."

For any Christian parent, but particularly for a pastor and his wife, this would be an unnerving moment. Fortunately, God gave these parents the self-control not to lash out. Instead, they simply let her talk, asking only an occasional question for clarification.

Later that night when they were alone, they discussed the situation. Realizing that God was not threatened by the pronouncement of a fifteen-year-old, they were glad they had let her talk. Several years later, she admitted it had all been a ploy to see if they would get angry. "I really appreciated the way you two hung in there with me when I acted that way," she said.

The pastor went on to explain that they had learned that night the power of gentleness to change a person's heart. "It may not happen immediately, but over time it does its work."

The late tennis pro, Arthur Ashe, also understood the power of a gentle response. In the 1970s, during the peak of his tennis career, he was locked in a tough battle against a verbally abusive opponent. From the other side of the net, this man taunted Ashe, cursed him, and mocked every move he made.

Two hours into the game, Ashe unexpectedly walked off the court. The line judge stopped him and said, "Mr. Ashe, if you leave the court, you will automatically forfeit the match."

Quietly he replied, "I'm close to losing my temper. I'd rather forfeit the match than my dignity." Then he walked toward the showers.

The next day, tennis officials reviewed the videotape. They were sickened by what they saw. It was clear that Ashe's opponent had deliberately tried to provoke him. And because of that player's unsportsmanlike conduct, they awarded the match to Ashe.

When Christians practice the uncommon grace of gentleness, we have more than good manners on our side. We have God. As the apostle Peter reminds us, "The eyes of the Lord are on the righteous and his ears are attentive to their prayer" (1 Peter 3:12).

Though others may not see, God sees. Though others may not hear, God hears. His eyes are sharper than any line judge's. His ears, keener than any official's. He's looking at us and listening to us, both on and off the court. What He's hoping to see in our conduct and hear in our conversations is gentleness.

CHAPTER 2

ATTENTIVENESS

For many years I jogged three or four times a week with David Davenport, a brilliant corporate attorney and former mayor of Plymouth (a suburb of Minneapolis where I lived) and one of my best friends. During those runs, we discussed the political issues of the day, the direction of our personal lives, and many other things. A bond grew between us as the miles rolled beneath our feet. I knew what made David laugh. I knew what made him cry. I knew what worried him and how his mind worked. He knew the same things about me.

Our conversations were often intense. When there was conflict, an energy passed back and forth between us. It worked its way from our tongues, down to our feet, and back up again. The faster we ran, the more intensely we talked, and that made us run even faster.

Neither of us would have admitted it then, but we both showed a lot of selfishness during those conversations. We often interrupted each other or finished one another's sentences because each of us knew what the other was going to say. This led to some pretty memorable conversations.

Those conversations came to a sudden end on Memorial Day weekend, 1993, when David's car was broadsided in a terrible automobile accident. In the medevac helicopter en route to the hospital, the flow of oxygen to David's brain was interrupted, and he suffered brain damage as a result. He still has partial use of his left hand, so he can feed himself, sign his name, and operate his computer, but apart from that he is a quadriplegic. His spirits are great, his mental abilities are as strong as ever, but his speech patterns are slower.

I would do anything for David, but when we talk, I still have to fight to keep from interrupting him. Sometimes it's all I can do to keep from answering his questions before he finishes asking them. I could blame my quick tongue or my love of mental give and take, but those excuses don't get to the heart of the matter.

The truth is, I interrupt because I like to control conversations. I want them to follow my agenda, to proceed at my pace, to end where I would like them to end. Because of that, I am quick to speak. And because of that, I am slow to listen. This is just the opposite of what the brother of our Lord tells us in James 1:19: "Be quick to listen, slow to speak." I wonder if James interrupted his brother as they were growing up. And I wonder if it was the cross Jesus bore that changed him—as it was the cross David had to bear that changed me.

This compulsion to be the god of our own conversational universe doesn't suddenly happen just to middle-aged jogging buddies. It's fixed in us from birth.

Illustrating this is a list of "Toddler Property Laws," which I saw hanging on the wall of the pediatric radiology department at the University of Arizona Hospital:

1. If I like it, it is mine.
2. If it is in my hand, it is mine.
3. If I can take it from you, it is mine.
4. If I had it a little while ago, it is mine.
5. If it is mine, it must never appear to be yours in any way.

6. If I'm doing something or building something, all
the pieces I need are mine.

7. If it looks just like mine, it is mine.

8. If I think it is mine, it is mine.

"It's mine" is something we stop saying when we reach adulthood, but the selfishness is still there and still central to who we are. One of the ways it surfaces is in weak listening skills. It's easy for us to talk, lecture, convince, and assume we have the best thoughts to share in any given situation. In the process, we miss out on a whole world of ideas that could enrich us.

Most of all, we miss out on the hidden depths and fascinating stories that exist in the lives of people all around us. God created these people in His image, and He expects us to honor them as His creation. We do that when we are attentive to them, when we take the time to listen to them, trying to understand not only *what* they are saying but *why* they are saying it.

Of course, it's easier to make snap judgments based on stereotypes than to engage a person in thoughtful conversation. It's hard work to understand someone else's point of view. It takes time and energy, things that are in short supply in our fast-paced society.

In the end, we must make a choice. We can look for excuses—our listening skills are weak, we don't have the right kind of training, we're naturally shy and fearful of deep conversations—or we can look for solutions.

Here are some solutions that can serve as guideposts to a lifetime of better listening.

GIVING UP THE NEED TO WIN

In this dog-eat-dog world, the puppies don't make it. Or so we are told. Winning is everything, and everyone who doesn't win is, by definition, a nothing. Or so we are told. It's as if we wake up each day at the starting gate and have to sprint to the finish line to reclaim our sense of worth. High-powered business people often reach the top of their professions by working a little longer and running just a little faster than the competition. They are trained to out-think, out-talk, and out-do everyone around them.

Is it any surprise they are the ones who fail to be good listeners?

Some time ago, I was watching a U.S. senator debate our foreign policy toward Mexico with an expert on Latin American affairs. A moderator was asking both of them questions. The senator always let the expert finish her answer before he spoke, but the expert did not extend the same courtesy. She acted as if her opinion was the only thing that mattered. She was totally focused on winning. She listened only long enough to formulate a strategy for her next attack.

Listening is a skill that is essential not only in debating but in decision-making. The CEO of an organization told me this story about a decision his board of directors made. His organization was growing rapidly, and they needed to expand their facilities. The most obvious site for their expansion was on a piece of vacant property located some distance from their main plant, but they were having a difficult time with some neighborhood groups opposed to the expansion. During the course of this ongoing debate, a piece of property next to the main plant became available.

In a board meeting, one of the directors suggested that this new piece of property was more than adequate for their needs. Using it would require them to negotiate with the city to give up part of a useless, dead-end street. This would be a much easier process than trying to satisfy the various neighborhood groups at the other location. Their old plant would have to be modified to fit in with the new building, but this alternative wasn't a major expense.

He had barely completed his proposal when a very vocal and negative board member attacked the idea. He called it foolish and without merit, insisting it would be too expensive. When his tirade was over, a shocked silence descended on the room. No one was willing to oppose him, and the idea was dropped without further discussion or research.

It was difficult for the CEO to tell me this story. I asked him why it was still such a painful memory after all these years. He paused to collect himself, then said,

> In retrospect, I was ashamed of myself and the other board members. We prided ourselves on being good listeners who discussed things rationally. But in this case, one negative person just overwhelmed us. Everyone seemed to lose his bearings. Nobody could bring himself to insist that we research the idea to see if it had merit. After it was too late to purchase the adjoining piece of property, we discovered that it would have met all our needs. We failed because we had violated our basic principles of listening to everyone and doing careful research. We capitulated to that bully, and our stockholders paid the price.

He paused. In his eyes I saw the depths of that old pain. In a quiet voice he added,

> I had grown so accustomed to abrasive and intimi-dating behavior that I missed it happening right in front of me. I was in charge. I should have known better.

For some, poor listening is the result of ignorance. Poor listeners move through life deaf to what others are saying. A friend in an athletic chaplaincy says that many successful athletes are poor listeners because they spend so many hours in solitude, honing their physical skills. In that environment their listening skills don't have a chance to develop. These men and women perform well and usually can speak well, but listening can be a real problem for them.

Many of us, though, know exactly what we're doing. We are like the board member who practiced winning through intimidation. In the heat of battle, we reach for the weapons of this world. We deliver powerful arguments, using every verbal tactic we know, and watch with great satisfaction as our opponents are driven from the field. What we don't recognize are the casualties of our fight for supremacy: compassion, kindness, dignity, respect, justice, truth, godliness.

In our rush to the front lines, we forget one of the most basic statements of Jesus about discipleship: "If anyone would come after me, he must deny himself and take up his cross daily and follow me" (Luke 9:23). "Take up your cross," Jesus said, not "take on your competition."

The situation becomes even more frightening when we intimidate in the name of Jesus and use "God talk" as just one more weapon in our arsenal. The longer I am part of the Christian subculture, the more I see Christian leaders whose desire to beat the competition is stronger than their desire to be like Christ.

Dr. Ray Burwick, a Christian counselor, says he has seen many Christian leaders with all the characteristics of an alcoholic. They fervently deny they have any problems, oblivious to what they are really doing. They have no idea how their actions are affecting those around them. Their addiction? Power. For them, the Bible is a sourcebook for sermons, not a guidebook for growth. Intoxicated with the swill of their own authority, they lack the self-awareness necessary to see themselves as they really are, as others see them, and as God sees them. Because of that, like the alcoholic in denial, they see no need to be a part of a Twelve Step program that could help them out of their own sin.

We begin our journey with Christ by confronting our sins. Alcoholics Anonymous meetings begin with the members confronting their sins in words like, "I'm Jill, and I'm an alcoholic." Wouldn't it be great in our Christian meetings if we could say, "I'm Jim, and I'm arrogant" or "I'm John, and I need the Savior"?

When we confess our sins and our need for a Savior, we are "saved," to use the biblical terminology. Though our salvation takes place in a moment of time, our sanctification progresses over a lifetime. It's an ongoing process, as the apostle Paul stated: "So then, just as you received Christ Jesus as Lord, continue to live in him" (Colossians 2:6). This ongoing self-awareness of sin and a willingness to change are necessary for the continued growth of Christ's life in ours (1 John 1:6-9). My friend Richard Hendrix says, "When I became a Christian, it was not just to have my sins forgiven but also to have my life become as close to that of Jesus Christ as possible."

If our drive to win is stronger than our desire to become like Christ, we will avoid the regular self-examination necessary for spiritual growth. This type of self-awareness prepares us to be aware of others. And in doing so, it prepares us to serve them.

"The Son of Man did not come to be served," Jesus said, "but to serve, and to give his life as a ransom for many" (Matthew 20:28). The ultimate expression of that service was shown at the cross. But Jesus not only died serving, He lived serving. The most vivid example of that was demonstrated in an Upper Room during the Last Supper. There He took on a job normally reserved for a household slave and washed His disciples' feet (John 13:1-17).

This was a necessary and much-appreciated service in an age of dirt roads covered with human refuse, animal droppings, and lots of dust. Foot washing was part of a host's duty to his guests because it relieved them of that daily accumulation of dirt and filth. It also provided welcomed relief from stiffness and fatigue for people who went most places by foot and who wore ordinary sandals, not orthopedic shoes.

The servant attitude of Jesus in foot washing suggests a pattern for the uncommon grace of attentiveness. By listening to others, we can help cleanse them of the burdens they have picked up during their daily journey through our crowded, complex, and competitive world. The battle cry of God's people should not be confused with the cry arising from that world. Ours is not "victory through intimidation" but "transformation through service."

We must regularly ask ourselves if our conversations live up to the servant attitude of Jesus. Do we take the time to understand what others are trying to tell us? Do we care enough to listen? Do we let them speak so they can unburden themselves, or do we rush in before they are done, jumping at conclusions, tossing in our two-cents-worth of advice, making sure we get in the last word?

The ethic in the kingdom of God is not "survival of the fittest" but "service to the neediest." We bring people into that kingdom by serving their needs. And one of their greatest needs is to speak what is in their hearts to someone who has a heart to listen.

Being Humble About Our Opinions

Once we have given up our need to win and have embraced the servant attitude of Jesus, we are well on our way to reaching another milestone on the road to being a good listener: being humble about our own opinions.

In Philippians 2:3, Paul encouraged us to be like Christ. He wrote, "Do nothing out of selfish ambition or vain conceit, but in humility consider others better than yourselves." Talking out of turn is one of the ways we express "selfish ambition or vain conceit." Listening displays the opposite of selfishness because it makes another person more important than ourselves. Any such act of humility allows the character of

Jesus to grow in our lives. Conversely, any act of pride stunts that growth.

I've spent much of my life in the academic world, a place that should stimulate growth but often stunts it. For all the years I've spent with them, I will never understand why many academics are such poor listeners. These people spend their whole lives learning to evaluate diverse arguments and contradictory evidence. You would think this training would make them particularly good listeners, but often that is not the case. The presence of "selfish ambition or vain conceit" can be a huge problem at colleges, universities, and seminaries.

For centuries Christian theologians have been trying to organize biblical knowledge into systems of belief that would answer our questions about God, the universe, and our place in it. Two of the major Protestant systems that have grown up since the Reformation are covenant theology and dispensationalism. Well-educated men and women who love God sincerely believe in each system. Inevitably, they have disagreed with each other and with those who believe in other theological systems. Sadly, though, these debates sometimes have been characterized by an unwillingness on either side to listen to what the other side is saying.

When I was in seminary, my theology professor did not accept covenant theology. In his attempt to show us the superiority of dispensationalism, he built up a series of straw men to represent covenant theology. Then he slashed and trashed, cut and burned, ridiculed and demeaned, until there was nothing left of the covenant viewpoint. He treated other Christian thinkers who held different views as enemies. He gave them no credit for wanting to find the truth or for being intelligent students of the Bible, and he encouraged his students to do the same.

Let me contrast his attitude with that of Dr. Kem Oberholtzer, vice president of Academic Affairs and professor of Biblical Literature at Phoenix Seminary, where I was president for two years. Kem is a dispensationalist, but when he got to the subject of covenant theology, he invited someone who holds that view to present it to the class. Kem is convinced about the correctness of his position, but that does not keep him from being fair toward those with whom he disagrees. Kem's attitude is the Christlike one.

People who work in churches and other Christian ministries often have the same trouble with differing viewpoints. A friend of mine, for example, was invited by one of the assistant pastors of another church to come to their pastors' conference. He declined. The next year another assistant pastor called with the same request. Again he declined. The third year the senior pastor called to ask why he would not come to speak at the conference.

My friend said, "You and I believe almost the very same things, but the people who disagree with us are good people. So when you quit saying, '*This* is what the Bible says,' and start saying, '*I believe* this is what the Bible says,' then I will come speak at your conference."

Admitting our limited understanding, especially in regard to spiritual truth, is a mark of humility. John Wesley said the proof of our imperfection is that we disagree about what the Bible says. There is nothing wrong with the Bible. What is wrong is how we perceive it. We perceive it with minds that are limited by our intelligence, with hearts that are clouded by our prejudice, and with souls that are damaged by our sin. These are what keep us from seeing the Bible clearly and constructing a perfect theology. And we should say, along with Paul, "Now we see but a poor reflection as in a mirror; then we shall see face to face. Now I know in part; then I shall know fully, even as I am fully known" (1 Corinthians 13:12).

When we admit we "know in part," then humility rather than pride, love rather than hate, respect rather than disrespect will mark our disagreements. And then maybe instead of just heat, our disagreements will begin generating a little light.

While living in England I found an old book of John Wesley's sermons. Since then, I have been challenged by something he wrote in the preface of the book. I think you will agree that these words written over two hundred years ago are words for our contemporary society and church.

> Are you persuaded you see more clearly than me? It is not unlikely that you may. Then treat me as you would desire to be treated yourself upon a change of circumstances. Point me out a better way than I have yet known. Show me it is so, by plain proof of Scripture. And if I linger in the path I have been accustomed to tread, and am therefore unwilling to leave it, labour with me a little; take me by the hand, and lead me as I am able to bear. But be not displeased if I entreat you not to beat me down in order to quicken my pace: I can go but feebly and slowly at best; then, I should not be able to go at all. May I not request of you, further, not to give me hard names, in order to bring me into the right way: Suppose I were ever so much in the wrong, I doubt this would not set me right. Rather, it would make me run so much farther from you, and so get more and more out of the way.
>
> Nay, perhaps, if you are angry, so shall I be too; and then there will be small hopes of finding the truth. If once anger arise, [like smoke], (as Homer somewhere expresses it), this smoke will so dim the eyes of my soul, that I shall be able to see nothing clearly.[1]

BEING WILLING TO ADMIT THAT WE MAY BE WRONG

A knock-down-drag-out debate was being fought in the editorial pages of a leading Christian magazine. The crowning moment came when one of the participants wrote that he had been misquoted by his opponent. With the misquote, communication broke down, and both sides stopped listening. I found myself sorry that he did not say, "maybe I miscommunicated," instead of assuming that he had been misquoted.

It was a tragic moment, tragic not only for the two people in the debate but for all the community of faith to whom the apostle Paul said, "in Christ we who are many form one body, and each member belongs to all the others" (Romans 12:5). "We're all in this together" is another way of saying it. And together we will help each other grow into the likeness of Christ, or together we will keep each other from growing. What we say to one another and how we say it can stimulate the roots of our spiritual life or poison them, just as what was said on the editorial page of that Christian magazine could have been encouraging instead of divisive.

It's easy to miss the significance of a misquoted or misunderstood statement. At first glance, it seems right to defend ourselves with a response like, "I didn't say that, and I don't want you claiming that I did." We are fighting back, we tell ourselves, because the truth is at stake. But we usually don't respond like that because we want to set the record straight. We respond like that because we are unwilling to admit we may have been mistaken or we may have misspoken. This hints at a serious problem—the problem of arrogance. It is a serious problem because arrogance makes listening, and the communication that flows from it, impossible.

Just as we need theological humility when it comes to Scripture, we need relational humility when it comes to speaking. We need to realize that communication is, at best, an imperfect science. Sometimes we intend to say one thing but something else comes out. Even when we get it right, others can easily misunderstand what we've said. To keep the lines of communication open, we have to admit that we will make mistakes and others will misunderstand us. Listening to criticism, even when it grows out of a misunderstanding, is one of the ways we have for showing others that we value them as God does.

If we truly want to communicate, we'll listen carefully to others, especially when they're trying to tell us what they thought they heard us say. When they misquote us, it is often effective to respond, "I don't think I said that, but if I did, I did not mean to say it. What I meant to say was . . . ." In a more formal setting, such as the debate just mentioned, we can offer to check an official record that both parties trust. That way we can determine exactly what was said or written. In either case, it is more important to listen to our critics respectfully than it is to prove our position indisputably.

CAREFULLY CONSIDERING OTHER PEOPLE'S WORDS

Good listening also requires that we shift the focus of our attention to the other person's words. This means that our reaction to his or her comments is less important than the content of those comments. We should never assume we know what someone else means. Such a judgment comes from pride, not humility, as the following incident illustrates.

A writer I know told me about a dispute he had with a man who is very proud of his reputation as an expert Bible interpreter. As they were discussing a point my friend had made in a speech, the expert insisted he knew exactly what my friend was trying to say.

"No, that's *not* what I was trying to say," my friend protested. He tried to explain, but the expert cut him off.

"You don't understand. I am an expert in interpretation, and this is certainly what you meant."

I shook my head at the absurdity of what I was hearing. "How did you deal with him?" I asked.

He shrugged. "I just figured he was an adolescent hiding out in an adult body. He's one of those brilliant fools who always has to be right. And he's not much use to anybody, because he doesn't know how to be a team player. Sure, he's intelligent, but it's a narrow, twisted sort of intelligence. Solomon warned us about those kinds of folks. You know the passage, 'Do not answer a fool according to his folly, or you will be like him yourself' (Proverbs 26:4). I didn't want to waste my time trying to fix this guy. I'll leave that to the psychologists."

If you think this is an extreme example of bad listening, consider how we typically treat the people around us. When we don't agree with the premise of someone's argument—or at least with some of the points being made—we usually stop listening. We may ignore him, waiting for the direction of the conversation to change. Or, if the issue is important to us, we may openly oppose what he is saying. In either case, the focus has shifted from what the other person is saying to what we think of it. We react like this because we want to remain secure in our own opinions.

But the price for that security is high. When we fail to listen to the opinions of others, we fall prey to our own opinions, which are often little more than extensions of our own egos. We also miss a perfect opportunity to proclaim the gospel, because most people will learn more about the love of Christ from our attentive silence than they ever will from our "expert" opinions.

RESISTING THE PRESSURE TO HAVE INSTANT ANSWERS

Once we focus on what others are saying, we begin to see the world through *their* eyes, to hear with *their* ears, to feel with *their* hearts. As their world becomes clearer to us, we begin to understand the things that concern them or cause them pain. This new way of seeing moves our heart to compassion, which, in turn, moves our lips and our hands and our feet to relieve their pain.

In our zeal to give help, though, we must be careful not to give instant answers. Instant answers inhibit dialogue, which is essential for gaining understanding. Solomon's ageless advice reminds us that "plans fail for lack of counsel, but with many advisers they succeed" (Proverbs 15:22). He also warned, "For lack of guidance a nation falls, but many advisers make victory sure" (Proverbs 11:14). Solomon's concern is not so much to encourage others by letting them talk as it is to protect us from our own ignorance. If we are not in the habit of considering viewpoints other than our own, we will make some very bad decisions. We are told to seek counsel, advisers, and guidance, which means we should be more intent on hearing others than on making ourselves heard.

The issues we face in today's society are much more complex than they were even a few decades ago. Most of us live with more fear and anxiety than ever before. We are bombarded with information—often contradictory—about moral issues, matters of public policy, new technologies, medical risks, environmental hazards, scandals, and institutional corruption that directly impacts our lives. There isn't time to absorb everything, much less to come up with a Christlike response to each and every issue. Add to that the pressure modern society places on us to have instant responses for everything, and it becomes even more critical that we take the time to consider different viewpoints—and to listen, *really* listen, to all of them.

Being Willing to Negotiate

It should be clear by now that listening is anything but passive. It requires great concentration. This is especially true when dealing with new ideas and differing viewpoints. Whether we are listening to support someone else or to find guidance for our own lives, we need to learn how to put all that information in perspective. To do that, we must be willing to negotiate.

Few people in this century have negotiated with more parties in hardened opposition to each other than Jimmy Carter has. Jim Wooten says this about the former President's negotiation style: "At the core of his approach—born at Camp David and honed, if not perfected, over the years in his dealings with some of the world's most unsavory rogues (from Ethiopia's Mengistu to Somalia's Aideed)—is a suspension of judgment on the people across the table. Whatever he knows or thinks he knows about them, unless he strips that from the emotional and intellectual context of their conversations, nothing will happen. 'That's the critical element of conflict resolution,' Carter says. 'The willingness to resist recriminations . . . and the patience to allow them enough time to understand that there's nothing on the table except a mutual effort to reach some sort of agreement.'"[2]

Too often we lose sight of our need to find common ground, especially in the midst of conflict. It is only as we add the art of negotiation to our listening skills that we can move forward in relationships where differences of opinion occur.

Dr. Ken Sylvester, president of the Organization Strategy Institute, is one of the leading experts in the United States on the subject of negotiation. Sylvester believes that most conflicts arise from a breakdown in communication, not from fundamental disagreements between people. This leads him to some strategies very different from those advocated by negotiation experts who hammer their opponents in order to achieve victory through intimidation.

Sylvester has observed that most conflicts intensify because those involved react to one another. This usually happens long before there is any understanding of the fundamental issues involved in the conflict. This process manifests itself in six major ways.

1. The atmosphere at the beginning of the conflict is already characterized by hostility, frustration, suspicion, or mistrust.
2. There is no real communication between the parties involved. They are unresponsive to comments made by the other side and treat each other as enemies.
3. The original issue, which may have been clear at the beginning, is now unclear. New issues and conflicts, created by the emotional responses of all parties, have clouded the initial issue.
4. Everyone focuses on disagreements rather than looking for points of agreement.
5. People "lock into" their positions and seek only to defend their point of view.
6. Each side is primarily driven by the emotion of the moment and the need to control the situation. There is no desire to move toward a resolution of the conflict or a solution to the original problem.

Sylvester goes on to suggest some principles for negotiation that also show us how to listen in the midst of a conflict.

1. Clarify any potential point of misinterpretation.
2. See if you can articulate the other person's point of view. This is the only way the other person will know for certain that you understand.
3. Break larger issues into smaller ones. This keeps emotional arguments and outbursts from controlling the discussion.
4. Find some common ground in the midst of the conflict, and get all parties to agree that it exists.
5. Emphasize integrity and behave in a trustworthy manner. Where there is trust, people will feel free to express themselves. This will make them more creative and productive. Without trust, people will be defensive, evasive, nonproductive, dishonest, and uncommunicative.[3]

When we have learned to seek common ground, even in the midst of conflict, then our listening skills can be the tools that build the bridge of reconciliation.

BECOMING RECONCILERS THROUGH COMPASSIONATE LISTENING

During His life on earth, Jesus repeatedly demonstrated that compassion could change people. Jesus recognized sin for what it was, but He never lost compassion for the sinner.

He shocked the sinful Samaritan woman simply by speaking to her, and then He listened to her questions carefully (John 4:4-26). He refused to condemn the woman caught in adultery (John 8:3-11), and He mourned over His people's refusal to accept Him as Messiah (Matthew 23:37).

We need to take seriously Christ's words to the religious leaders who criticized Him for socializing with sinners: "Go and learn what this means: 'I desire mercy, not sacrifice.' For I have not come to call the righteous, but sinners" (Matthew 9:13). Many of us who are followers of Jesus are far too worried about the lifestyles and values of other people. We have forgotten that God did not give us a ministry of conviction but of reconciliation.

Paul eloquently described this ministry in 2 Corinthians:

Therefore, if anyone is in Christ, he is a new creation; the old has gone, the new has come! All this is from God, who reconciled us to himself through Christ and gave us the ministry of reconciliation: that God was reconciling the world to himself in Christ, not counting men's sins against them. And he has committed to us the message of reconciliation. We are therefore Christ's ambassadors, as though God were making his appeal through us. We implore you on

Christ's behalf: Be reconciled to God. God made him
who had no sin to be sin for us, so that in him we
might become the righteousness of God. (5:17-21)

It is easy for us to forget that our walk with Jesus is just that:
a walk, a step-at-a-time journey that spans not only distance but
time. People don't change overnight but over a lifetime. And
we must be as patient toward them in the time it takes them to
change as we want them to be toward us—and as Jesus *is*
toward us.

Some time ago, I was having dinner with my longtime
friend, Dr. John Aker. We were carrying on a polite and ani-
mated conversation with our server, Frankie, when the discussion unexpectedly took a serious turn. This young woman
began to share a very painful part of her past with us. Five
years earlier, as a single woman of twenty, she had given birth
to a little girl named Maddie and then had chosen to give the
baby up for adoption. We were surprised not only by Frankie's
willingness to discuss this with us, but also by the fact that she
claimed to have a pro-choice view on abortion.

John and I are both pro-life, so we are quite familiar with
the use of adoption as a solution for unwanted pregnancies,
but it had never occurred to us that a pro-choice person might
choose life. My friend asked Frankie how adoption fit in with
her pro-choice views.

Frankie answered, "I believe that pro-choice means just
what it says—that you have the right to choose." She then
explained how she had arranged a very open adoption so her
baby would get the best of care and so she could still have
some contact with her. Frankie hopes that in this way the child
will never have to wonder who her birth parents are or what
the circumstances of her adoption were. Frankie has continued to have a very healthy relationship with Maddie's adoptive parents and sees the little girl whenever she returns to her
hometown.

John and I were struck by the reasonableness of Frankie's solution and her concern for the welfare of the child—things we wouldn't have expected from a pro-choice person. Soon the three of us were discussing the negative expectations that both sides in the abortion debate have for each other. We concluded that each side needs an enemy to hate in order to keep the passion for their own position at a white-hot level. This certainly goes a long way toward explaining the violence and lack of rational discussion that surround much of the abortion issue.

"Things have gotten so hostile lately," Frankie said with a sigh, "and just when we need to be listening to one another the most. Violence doesn't solve anything—it just leads to more violence. Until we start listening to each other and really start communicating, there won't be any resolution of this conflict."

Her words bring a message to us all. It's only as we take the time to listen to people that we will begin to understand why they speak and act the way they do.

Are we willing to take that time?

Jesus did. With the Samaritan woman in the middle of the day. With Nicodemus in the middle of the night. And with us whenever we've needed to talk. He takes the time with us to be there, to listen, to respond. He comes to us with compassion, not condescension—as a reconciler, not a reactionary.

Do we really want to be like Jesus?

That's the *real* question, isn't it?

For if we become like Him, it will change not only the way we live; it will change the way we listen.

CHAPTER 3

LOYALTY

W HEN MY FATHER WAS DYING OF A BRAIN TUMOR THAT HAD severely affected his speech and motor skills, none of us in the family knew how much time he had left. But we understood the importance of getting his signature on some papers in his safe-deposit box while he was still mentally competent. The president of the bank, Dean Cottrell, was a long-time friend of Dad's, so I called him to make the necessary arrangements.

I will never forget the scene. Dad sat in the vault on a stool. Mr. Cottrell knelt down next to him to open the safe-deposit box. As he knelt there, Dad patted him on the shoulder—and said in his halting voice, "My friend." It was an act of tremendous love and a testimony to years of friendship. Since he could no longer speak clearly or well, my dad found another way to say goodbye, to thank him for his help that day and for his friendship in the past. Dad's touch and two words spoke volumes!

Whenever I think of that day in the bank, I am reminded of the words of Solomon in Proverbs 18:24: "A man of many companions may come to ruin, but there is a friend who sticks closer than a brother." What is it that distinguishes the friend who is like a member of the family? In a word, loyalty.

Loyalty makes us stay close to someone who is facing trouble when others are too busy, too tired, too embarrassed, or too frightened to maintain contact. Loyalty is about deeds, not only words. Its presence or absence forms one of the truest tests of our relationships with each other. It does not appear suddenly. It is developed over a long period of time, often at great cost. Of all the uncommon graces, it is the one that is the hardest to counterfeit.

It was from England that I voted in my first American election. It was an exciting time for me. I loved the photograph of President-elect Nixon and Vice-President-elect Agnew standing together with huge smiles on their faces. Nixon was grasping Agnew's hand as they thrust their hands into the air in a victory salute. The picture was everywhere: On all three television networks. On the front page of every local newspaper. On the cover of every national news magazine. And on the covers of newspapers in England, where Susan and I were living. It gave me a sense of security that I had voted for the winners and that they were such committed friends.

But the picture turned out to be a fraud. The friendship was an act. And the loyalty I thought was there, wasn't. I never knew that, though, until President Nixon's funeral. It was then that I, along with the rest of the country, learned that from the time of Agnew's resignation until Nixon's death, the two of them had talked in private only three times. During the time between that election victory and Agnew's resignation, their friendship was a lie; the picture, simply a photo-op for the press.

What was it that my father and his banker had that Nixon and Agnew didn't? Loyalty.

The Characteristics of Loyalty

Loyalty involves serving others
Like all the uncommon graces, loyalty begins with God.

Though we live in a fallen world where terrible things

sometimes happen, God is trustworthy, in control, and faithful in sustaining us, causing His sun to rise on the evil and the good and sending rain on the righteous and the unrighteous (Matthew 5:45).

God's loyalty not only sustains us, it seeks us. In the life of Christ we see this seeking quality at work, striving to save those who were lost, leaving the ninety-nine sheep that were safe and going after the one sheep that strayed. The apostle Paul reminds us that our redemption is possible only because Jesus left heaven to seek us, laying aside His equality with God in order to take on the role of a servant (Philippians 2:5-8).

His behavior is a model for our own. Jesus does not set us free from sin so we can live a life of self-indulgence. Paul spells this out for us when he says, "You, my brothers, were called to be free. But do not use your freedom to indulge the sinful nature; rather, serve one another in love" (Galatians 5:13).

"Our willingness to serve others," suggests my good friend Gene Bourland, pastor of First Evangelical Free Church in Minneapolis, "is a practical test of our spiritual maturity and a living proof of our love for God." The loyalty of God not only seeks us, serves us, and sustains us, it also cycles through us to others. It's like the rain falling from heaven to water the earth, causing seeds to germinate, plants to grow, flowers to bloom, and branches to bear fruit. In our case, the Spirit of God is the rain that descends, bringing forth the fruit. It is the fruit that attracts others to take and eat—fruit that looks and smells and tastes remarkably like Jesus.

Loyalty grows out of intimacy

In order for loyalty to develop, we must be committed to serving one another.

Service by itself doesn't create loyalty. A former Secretary of State said that, while in office, he was besieged by people who were eager to spend time with him. Many of them would have been eager to announce that he was an important friend of theirs. But he had no illusions about those relationships. He knew that the day after he left office most of the people who desperately wanted to talk to him while he was Secretary of State wouldn't be returning his phone calls.

The relationship they wanted with the Secretary was defined by the service he could provide. Their loyalty would last as long as his term of office. That's because the relationship was born out of expedience, not intimacy. Loyalty can grow in our relationships only if we are also willing to cultivate intimacy. In our frenetic society, it is difficult to invest the amount of time necessary to achieve this goal. The process will be easier for us if we have some idea of the stages relationships pass through on the way to real intimacy.

Most of our relationships begin with "How do you do?" and many of them never progress beyond that. These are the people we know by name and greet with a smile and occasional small talk, but we know them only superficially. If they are people we work with, we may have a little more information about them because we have been in meetings together, worked on the same projects, attended the same office parties. Still, these are simply acquaintances. Neither of us makes a lasting impression on the other. *We may call them friends, but in reality they are no more than acquaintances.*

Then there are the people we know a little better. Most of us would call them friends. With them, we got past "How do you do?" long ago, but we never seem able to go beyond "What shall we do next?" These are the people we call when we want someone to join us in an activity. We hunt or fish with them, golf or bowl with them, share movies together or go to lunch. Sometimes our families spend time going places and doing things with their families. We may even share cultural events or church activities, which we might normally expect to generate a deeper relationship. Yet somehow we never get around to discussing anything very personal. We have no real connection to the lives of these people beyond the activities we share. *We may call these people friends, but in reality they are no more than pals.*

I have a friend who understands the limitations of these activity-oriented relationships. Dr. David Fisher is a serious motorcycle rider who puts thousands of miles a year on his bike. Though he enjoys the time riding with his friends, he has this to say about the experience: "Riding is the ultimate 'guy thing' because you can spend all day with your friends without any need to talk with them." (However, they do talk at night after the ride is completed.)

These relationships have more of an impact on us than the ones we have with simple acquaintances. They offer entertainment, if not enrichment. In relationships like this there are strict, unspoken limits as to how deeply we can share in one another's lives. Because of that, there is little opportunity for growth.

Please don't misunderstand me. I'm not saying it's wrong to have relationships centered around the activities we enjoy. In fact, it's normal, especially in the early stages of a relationship. But it's not normal for all of our relationships to remain at these levels. And it's not healthy. We need genuine friendships. Deep, nurturing friendships. And we need them desperately. *Genuine friends are people with whom we have some degree of intimacy.*

Intimate friendships are built on a foundation of intimate questions: *How are you different today than you were yesterday? What do you really want out of life? How do you feel right now? What do you think? What are your hopes . . . your dreams . . . your fears?* People with whom we can ask such questions are the people Solomon described when he wrote, "Wounds from a friend can be trusted" and "As iron sharpens iron, so one man sharpens another" (Proverbs 27:6,17). These relationships are the ones God uses to shape us into the image of His Son. They are channels of grace, true sacraments in the most literal sense of the word.

In his wonderful little book *Secrets*, Dr. Paul Tournier says that having secrets is an important part of being human. When we share them with others, those same secrets have the power to strengthen relationships as few other things have the power to do. Intimate friends are the ones with whom it is safe to share such secrets.[1]

Jesus Himself had varying levels of relationships with people, from acquaintances to intimate friends. His twelve disciples were certainly close to Him, but closer still were the inner circle of Peter, James, and John. The most intimate secret Jesus shared with them was not the death He was about to experience but the doubts He had about His ability to endure it. As Jesus wrestled with His fate in the Garden of Gethsemane, He called upon His three most intimate friends to share in the struggle by supporting Him in prayer (Matthew 26:36-46). It was a tremendous risk. It was also a tremendous act of loyalty.

When the disciples fell asleep, it was the loyalty Jesus felt for them that prompted Him to rebuke them for failing to uphold their end of the friendship (verses 40-41). This not only illustrates the power of loyalty to bring people closer, but also suggests another of its characteristics: honesty.

LOYALTY CANNOT SURVIVE WITHOUT HONESTY

I had fourteen terrific years pastoring a church in the suburbs of Minneapolis. It was a wonderful time of spiritual development, both for the congregation and for me. Part of the reason was that my time there began with a brutally honest evaluation of the congregation and the community. To accomplish this, we hired a church-growth expert from outside the area.

One of the things he told me in private still shocks me to this day: "The people here appreciate your teaching skills, but they will only comment on your bad sermons. They won't say anything when you do a good job. Most of them are white-collar professionals who are used to paying for top-quality services in their daily lives, and they expect the best from their church."

My first instinct was to tell him he was wrong. Then I started to think about how I treated the Sunday school teachers who cared for my kids. I expected them to do a good job, and it seldom occurred to me to express how grateful I was for their hard work.

Explaining this, the consultant pointed out how the culture of Minneapolis was heavily influenced by its large Scandinavian population. People with that ancestry formed a clear majority in our church. Scandinavians are not known for their exuberance of expression. In fact, one of my favorite jokes goes, "You've all heard about the Norwegian who loved his wife *so much* that he almost told her."

The church reflected the personalities both of its professional population and its ethnic population. That was something I needed to know if we were to succeed in coming together as a body and growing together into the fullness of Christ. The church succeeded in that goal because early in our relationship with each other, we confronted the issue honestly. That honesty laid the foundation for loyalty in those relationships. The two go hand in hand.

LOYALTY LEADS TO PERSONAL GROWTH

Loyalty in relationships creates an environment where mutual influence is possible. When I look back on the relationship between my father and his banker, I am amazed at how much they affected each other's lives.

One of the most striking areas had to do with spiritual issues. My father was a solid evangelical Christian, who took his faith very seriously. His friend was a Mormon, who was also serious about his faith but who didn't agree with Dad on the deity of Christ. They talked about their differences for years and were never able to agree on some very fundamental issues. Their friendship endured, though, because of their loyalty to each other. The end result was tremendous growth for both of them.

How many of us would have the courage to maintain such a close relationship with someone whose approach to such an important issue was so different from our own? There is an important truth here: The stronger our commitment to loyalty, the greater differences the relationship can endure and the greater growth it can experience.

It takes a lot of energy to live like this. That is why we usually avoid relationships with those who are very different from us. Such friendships cost a great deal. But investing only in relationships with people who are just like us costs a great deal, too. And the price is often a debit against our own spiritual development.

The Benefits of Loyalty

Many of us are adept at hiding the truth about our lives from those around us. We can become so proficient at this that we actually deceive ourselves. Sometimes we even try to fool God. One of the benefits of having loyal friends is that they have a way of bringing us out of hiding. But sometimes the person we've kept in hiding is Jesus. And sometimes a friend is the best one to bring Him out.

I'm thinking of three friends in particular, all of them ministers: Dr. John Aker, Dr. Dennis Baker, and Dr. David Fisher. We're all pretty busy and are usually only able to see each other once a year. Between those meetings we spend a lot of time on the phone. We don't keep many secrets from each other, and we can be pretty tough on each other at times. We enjoy one another's company, but we also have allowed God to change each of us through the influence of the others. It has taken hard work over the years to maintain these relationships, but I have never once regretted the time I have invested in them, or the time they have invested in me. For example, once John went with me to scout out a new car. Since John has had plenty of experience buying and selling cars, he quietly kept pushing me to be more aggressive in negotiating with the salesmen. Toward the end of my negotiations with one of them, something came over me. I was like a shark caught up in a feeding frenzy for the lowest price. And I was eating the salesman alive.

When the salesman left his office to discuss my latest demand with his sales manager, John turned to me and said, "Vawter, you drive a harder bargain than I do. You're cutting this guy off at the knees." The quiet intensity in his voice caught me off guard. He continued, "Remember, you didn't stop being a follower of Jesus when you walked through the door of this guy's office."

His words stopped me in my tracks. I had been competing—not representing Christ. I spent the next few minutes thinking about how I had treated the salesman. I wasn't very proud of what I discovered. When he came back, I made a conscious effort to treat him with more gentleness and respect.

It was the loyalty of my friend, John, that reminded me who I was hiding on the other side of that competitive exterior. Showing the salesman something of Christ was more important than getting a rock-bottom price. In the end, I got a good car at a fair price. And in the end, I didn't walk out of there with any scars on my soul or any teethmarks on the salesman.

THE LIMITS OF LOYALTY

Loyalty is not blind. It insists on knowing the truth. And sometimes the truth demands that we walk away from a relationship.

As a pastor, I've counseled a number of people who were converted to Christianity from the drug culture. Their conversions put them on a spiritual path that was at odds with the choices of their friends who were still using drugs. Many of them wanted to maintain their relationships with these people out of a sincere desire to help them. These new believers had discovered a way out of their dead-end life, and they wanted to share that way with their friends. What could be more loyal than that?

In most cases, though, these friends didn't want a way out. A spiritual path, wherever it led, didn't interest them. In fact, they resented it because it led their friends away from them.

These new Christians often agonized about abandoning their friends. As one who was responsible for nurturing these new believers, I was worried that their entanglement with these old relationships would choke out the emerging growth in their relationship with Christ. In order for their roots to take hold, most of them had to break off those friendships. A few of them, though, actually did convince some of their friends to turn to Christ. But all of them struggled with the question: What does it mean to be a loyal friend?

Loyalty places certain demands on a friendship. For them, it demanded that they try to help their friends escape the drug culture. But if their friends refused, loyalty demanded they walk away. This is a case of loyalty at the crossroads. On the one road was their loyalty to the relationship with their friends. Intersecting that road was their loyalty to their relationship with Christ. Jesus is the true way and the only way to life. Therefore, loyalty to Him was the highest obligation. Our loyalty to our friends demands that we show them the way as clearly and as convincingly as we can. But if they don't accept the way, sometimes it's best to be on our way, which is exactly what Jesus told His disciples to do when He sent them out in pairs to preach the gospel. If a town will not welcome you, He said, "shake the dust off your feet when you leave, as a testimony against them" (Mark 6:11).

A friend of mine who is a pastor spent many years getting to know another pastor in his town. They became close friends, both personally and professionally. Gradually, though, their friendship deteriorated. The problem began when they started sharing frustrations about their respective ministries. Neither of them was particularly interested in resolving their frustrations; they merely wanted to vent them. But like the duct work of a central heating system, these vents extended to every area of their relationship. Soon the sharing of their hurt, their anger, their fear, and their frustrations degenerated to gossip.

After a few months, my friend realized what was happening. He talked to his friend, suggesting they eliminate all cynicism from their conversations. Instead of accepting this challenge, the friend turned on him, calling him "holier than thou" and many other demeaning names.

Shortly afterward, my friend heard that this pastor was spreading hurtful rumors about his ministry. My friend realized that this relationship had become a blight on his relationship with Christ, and if he wanted to keep growing, he would have to remove it. There was nothing disloyal about his choice. In fact, it was an expression of loyalty to the original spirit of their friendship, for the intent of the friendship was to help each other grow in their relationship with Christ. His loyalty to Christ forced him to end the relationship.

Relationships grow in all sorts of ways, and not all of those ways are healthy. Sometimes they grow in ways that entangle us. Sometimes they grow in ways that infect us. Sometimes they simply grow apart, like the relationship I had with a man who had a great influence on me during college.

We were very close in those days and shared from the deep places of our lives. After I finished college, we lost touch with each other for a while. When we finally got together again, our time together was different. *We* were different. Our professional lives had grown in different directions; so had our spiritual lives. It wasn't that either of us had done anything wrong. We simply weren't interested in the same things anymore. I was deeply grieved about the loss of that friendship.

If loyalty to each other's growth is at the core of your friendships, when you come back and see a stump where there once towered a tree, you become sad. Once we had so much in common. Now all we have in common is our past. And although I'm thankful for the memories, I'm regretful that memories are all I have.

LOYALTY'S FINEST HOUR

Loyalty is proven by adversity. And its finest hour is in battle or stressful situations.

Fiercely fought battles are part of the histories of institutions as well as of nations. During my first year at Trinity Seminary, the vice-president disagreed with the president on the direction the school should take for the future. A few days after the disagreement became public, I saw the vice-president and asked how he was doing.

"I'm fine, John," he said, "but you need to know that I've resigned."

I was so shocked I couldn't think of anything to say. Then I asked him, "Are you sure you're doing the right thing?"

"You know as well as I do that vice-presidents have to be in step with their presidents," he answered. "Our friendship is still fine, but for conscience's sake I had to resign."

Sometimes the finest hour is not how heroic we are in defending our cause but how honorable we are in surrendering it. The vice-president knew that the short-term casualty of going to war might be the friendship and that the long-term casualty might be the strength of the institution. The casualty of not being honest with himself would be his conscience. Because of his loyalty to all three, he decided his job would be the casualty instead. It was a hard decision but a loyal one—loyal to the friendship, to his institution, and to his integrity. Now, twenty-five years later, all three are stronger than ever.

Sometimes the impassioned words of a loyal friend can turn the tide for us. Consider a friend and colleague of mine,

Steve Griffith, director of development at Phoenix Seminary. Once an executive vice-president of a major bus company, he was deeply frustrated with some things going on in the company. After voicing these frustrations to a Christian woman in the company, she replied with a stern admonishment:

"Look, Steve, you're not doing much of a job of living out your faith here. You may not like what your boss is doing, but God placed him in authority over you, and you have no right to talk behind his back."

Hard words to say. Hard words to hear. But because she was loyal enough to the friendship to say them—and Steve, loyal enough to hear them—the truth of those words turned the tide in his conflict with his boss.

A victory for him, for the company, and, more importantly, for the cause of Christ.

No cause was more strategic to Christ than the cross. No communication was more vital to Him than making sure His men understood that. Loyalty to His troops demanded no less.

Consider His loyalty to Peter, for example, and Peter's to Him. In the sixteenth chapter of Matthew, Peter stands firm in his conviction that Jesus is "the Christ, the Son of the living God" (verse 16). In response, Jesus makes one of the strongest statements on loyalty recorded anywhere in the Bible: "You are Peter, and on this rock I will build my church, and the gates of Hades will not overcome it" (verse 18).

Now that the disciples understand who Jesus really is, He tells them why He really came—to die (verse 21). The words shake Peter to the core of his commitment to Christ, and he won't hear of such a thing. He is appalled with the idea of Jesus handing Himself over to be killed (verse 22). "Over my dead body" captures the essence of his reply.

The mood suddenly shifts. So does the tone of Jesus' voice. His words are the strongest ever spoken to a disciple: "Get behind me, Satan! You are a stumbling block to me; you do not have in mind the things of God, but the things of men" (verse

23). These hard words are spoken to the very person He had praised so highly only a moment before. Jesus refuses to compromise His mission. He also refuses to let Peter fall short of his potential, or to let the other disciples misunderstand the cost of the gospel (verses 24-28). The loyalty Jesus felt for Peter demanded that He tell him the truth, regardless how hard the words that were necessary to convey it.

What was the result of those hard words? They led to those recorded in Acts chapter 2. After the Holy Spirit came on the day of Pentecost, Peter stood up and explained to the startled crowd that a new era of grace had been inaugurated by the death and resurrection of Jesus Christ—the very event Peter had once so vigorously opposed.

Sometimes the loyal words of a friend are hard to hear, hitting us like bricks. But sometimes those very bricks pave the road that leads us, as it did Peter, to our finest hour.

CHAPTER 4

CANDOR

WHEN OUR TWO CHILDREN WERE PRESCHOOLERS, THEY OFTEN left the living room with toys scattered everywhere. Throw in a hyperactive Sheltie dog named Laddie, and you might as well have declared it a disaster zone and called in the National Guard. One day when I could hardly see the floor for all the toys, I told them, "Okay, kids, we need to pick up this mess. Now whose toys are these?"

I was answered by two innocent-looking shrugs.

"I didn't do it," Stephanie said.

"Not me, Dad," Michael chimed in.

"Well, I know your mom didn't scatter these toys around, and I know I didn't," I said, "so that leaves just one other possibility. Laddie must have done it."

Two little heads immediately began to bob. "Yeah, that's right," they agreed. "Laddie did it."

Amazing, isn't it? Even as children, we're adept at hiding the truth in order to protect ourselves. As we grow older, we become a little more altruistic, sometimes hiding the truth to protect others. Such evasiveness, though, can have the opposite effect, especially when it involves the truth about someone you love, like your own father.

I loved my father a great deal. His name was Harry. He was a great father, a marvelous friend, and a wonderful example. That is why it was so difficult for me to watch his health deteriorate so suddenly because of a brain tumor. What made that experience even more difficult was the evasiveness of his neurosurgeon. I wanted to know the truth about my dad's prognosis. I *needed* to know the truth. But the doctor wouldn't tell me. Then one day I asked him point blank.

"Is he going to die?"

The doctor hesitated, then stepped around the question with an ambiguous answer and started down the hall. Not satisfied with his lack of candor, I caught up with him and stood in his way. Only then, when he couldn't get around me, did I finally get some answers. Later I asked my brother, Michael, who is a cardiologist, why the surgeon was reluctant to tell me the truth.

"Doctors sometimes hate to give people bad news," he replied. "But still, he wasn't being fair to you."

It's not just doctors who try to protect themselves and others from hard truths. When answers are difficult, most of us are uncomfortable giving them. That's why one of the uncommon graces believers need to practice with each other is candor — a commitment to giving each other honest answers, regardless how difficult or uncomfortable this is.

THIS TIME I'M TELLING THE TRUTH

The lack of candor in our society is pervasive. Some used-car lots now put stickers in their windows that read, "Important: Spoken promises are difficult to enforce. Ask the dealer to put all promises in writing."

The same stickers could be placed on the windows of the political machines that drive the country. It is no secret that growing numbers of Americans trust government and those who govern us less and less.

Lack of candor shows up on the advertising lot as well. An article appearing in the Minneapolis StarTribune revealed that a local monastery had been misleading the public about its famous bakery. "For decades, Minnesotans have bought 'Johnny Bread' believing it was made by Benedictine monks at St. John's Abbey at Collegeville—with some profits going to the university."[1] In truth, the article discloses, very little of the bread is baked on site. Since the 1950s, the monastery has sent its mix to outsiders, and the bread currently is produced at several sites around Minnesota. What little bread is baked in the monastery is neither mixed nor kneaded by the monks.

Consumers outside Minnesota face similar misrepresentations. I drove into the parking lot at the post office one day after I saw a huge sign that read, "Guaranteed service in five minutes or less." I later called the post office and asked, "What does your sign mean?"

"Uh, we will have you to the window in five minutes."

"Or what?"

"I'd better let you talk to the manager," was the answer. The manager explained that five minutes is a guideline they were trying to achieve. It turned out that "guaranteed service" wasn't a guarantee, only a goal.

Perhaps the spirit of our times was best expressed by Bob Arum, a boxing promoter. He reportedly used these words to explain to a boxer's manager why the contract he was offering was different from the one he originally promised: "Yesterday I was lying, but today I'm telling the truth."[2]

A Culture of Deceit

For years the Soviet regime allowed only two official newspapers: *Pravda,* which means "truth," and *Izvestia,* which means "news." The Russian people, known for their dark humor, said this about the newspapers: "There's no truth in *Pravda* and no news in *Izvestia*."

We have developed a similar cynicism in the United States. Though we enjoy constitutionally protected freedom of expression, some observers suggest we are living in a "culture of deceit." Maybe it is not much different from the culture Solomon lived in when he said, "An honest answer is like a kiss on the lips" (Proverbs 24:26). I think he's saying that it's rare when we get one, but when we do, it's exhilarating.

Nowhere is honesty such a rarity as in Washington, D.C. John Danforth, the distinguished senator serving there from Missouri, had this to say about one of his colleagues: "Senator Al Simpson from Wyoming is one of my favorite senators. Very tall, very skinny, very thoughtful, very funny. He has one characteristic that is not universally shared by politicians. He says exactly what he thinks with force and spirit and with no apparent concern for the consequences."[3] In other words, Simpson is a man of candor.

Practiced with love and discretion, candor strengthens rather than weakens relationships. It convinces us that other people care, that our friendship matters. When others are candid, they give us the opportunity to grow in our personal lives and develop character. We also gain a certain freedom of mind because we never have to worry if the person is telling us the truth, or if the person is saying one thing to us and something else to others.

FIRST CHURCH OF THE RUN-AROUND

It is one thing for our culture to avoid candor. It's another thing entirely for the church. Of all places you would expect the truth to be spoken—loudly, clearly, unequivocally—it would be there. Often, though, it isn't.

Not long ago I received a phone call from a pastor who

attended a seminary class I taught. He told me he was really hurting. I asked why.

"Because a prominent couple in my church just left," he explained.

"Why?"

"Because they said I'm impatient and unkind."

"Did they come to see you first?"

"No. They just talked with some other people about me and came to the conclusion that I lack patience and kindness."

"Did you go to them?"

"Yes. I asked them, 'Have I ever mistreated you or been short with you?' 'No,' they answered, 'but we've heard you're that way.'"

This pastor went on to explain that the woman had once worked in the church office, but she had quit almost a year earlier. Her explanation was that she wanted to be able to travel with her husband on business.

"So she lied to you," I said.

"Yes. She finally admitted she wanted me to be more like her former pastor. He would put his arm around people and say, 'How are you doing?' I'm more reserved, and she resents that."

This pastor hadn't been told the truth for more than a year. When the woman should have talked with him, she talked to others instead. And by the time he finally learned of her concerns, she had already left the church.

Lay people aren't the only ones who are evasive. Pastors sometimes are, too. One pastor, for example, insisted to the elder board that allegations of sexual impropriety against him were false. Then the elders played him a tape of telephone conversations his mistress had secretly recorded when she sensed he was about to dump her.

Not all allegations against the church's leadership are true, however. For example, a pastor friend of mine was alleged to be having an affair with his secretary. Someone spread the rumor to people in several other parts of the country, and soon the gossip mills were adding second shifts. Imagine the grief this caused my friend, a person of such integrity that he avoids any appearance of evil so thoroughly that he won't even ride in a car alone with any woman other than his wife or daughters.

One courageous person decided to get to the bottom of the allegations. After interviewing several people, he finally located the source of the rumor. He telephoned the person and took copious notes. He then arranged for a meeting with my accused friend and confronted him with the charges, which my friend flatly denied. The person conducting the investigation then went back to the accuser. This time, however, the accuser denied ever making the charges.

"So these three pages of notes I took of our conversation are just a dream," the investigator said, "because you and I never talked?"

"I never said anything to you about it," came the reply.

In each of these cases, the lack of candor devastated several people and threatened to hurt entire churches.

WHY WE PLAY HIDE AND SEEK

Why are we so reluctant to be candid with one another? I'd like to suggest several reasons.

The first reason we're reluctant to be candid is fear. If I tell someone the truth, I run the risk of being rejected. Because the truth is not always pleasant, it is not always welcome. One man told me he would not speak his mind at a church business meeting because "I want to keep having coffee with my friends."

A pretty high price for coffee, if you ask me.

Nice, amiable people are particularly good at the game because they crave harmony. That's why they sometimes tolerate phony relationships. They would rather keep the discord to a minimum than work through the noise to make music. But *keeping* the peace is not the task Jesus gave us. *Making* the peace *is*.

The second reason we are reluctant to be candid is that sometimes it's difficult. Because of that, we hide behind rationalizations. But hide and seek with the truth is no game the church should be playing, for every time we do, we disobey the clear teaching of Scripture: "Each of you must put off falsehood and speak truthfully to his neighbor, for we are all members of one body" (Ephesians 4:25).

A friend of mine once received a phone call from someone who wanted to complain about his pastor's theology. My friend listened for a moment, then said, "There's a high road or a low road you can take here. The low road would be to talk behind his back and rally opposition. The high road would be to talk with him. If that doesn't resolve your concerns, then use the official channels available to bring grievances to the board."

"I didn't really want to hear that," the person replied. "But you're right. I'm going to take the high road." He kept his word. As a result, the situation was resolved without splitting the church.

The third reason we're reluctant to be candid is our need to win. I've observed, particularly among leaders, that the truth is not always as important as the triumph. Winning for them is a strong motivation. And often the stronger the leader, the stronger the need to win. These people will protect their egos at any cost—even at the cost of compromising truth. Their greatest fear is being shown up by someone else. They will punish others rather than accept the blame. Deep down, they believe the philosophy that is reflected in a sign seen posted in a factory: "Notice from management: The beatings will cease when morale improves."

The fourth reason we're reluctant to be candid is our human nature. Human nature is fallen. It's our nature to be deceptive, a nature we inherited from our first parents. When God confronted them in the Garden of Eden about their disobedience, Adam blamed Eve, and Eve in turn blamed the serpent. Neither admitted the truth. Tacitly, though, they did.

They admitted their guilt by covering themselves with fig leaves. And we've been covering for ourselves ever since.

Just take a look at the fig leaf on this naked lie. It came through the mail from someone trying to sell fund-raising services. In his brochure he quoted a pastor who claimed that after he tried the plan, the giving in his church shot up by several thousand dollars a week. Perhaps it did, but it must have been several years ago because I know that church, and it is in financial straits.

Or consider the couple who led a marriage enrichment conference on the weekend, then on Monday morning announced they were getting a divorce.

To counteract all the cover-ups, we need people who can see past the fig leaves. We need people with the backbone of prophets who have the courage to stand up and say, "This isn't right. We're not dealing with the truth here. Please give me the straight story."

One college board chairman told an administrator, "I don't want you going out and conducting any more conflict-resolution seminars. You haven't resolved a single conflict in our own institution." That's a hard word. But it's the right word, the word of a prophet. And it's the type of word that's needed in today's society.

The Dangers and Benefits of Honesty

There *are* dangers to practicing candor. People offended by the truth or reluctant to deal with the truth may talk behind your back. You may find yourself rejected by the in-group or the elite, who may not appreciate so much integrity. Or you may find yourself isolated or losing a position of influence because you said too much.

While there are disadvantages to practicing candor, the advantages outweigh them. You maintain your integrity, which is one advantage. Your family respects you, which is another. You can sleep at night without anxiety. You can look at yourself in the morning without shame. You don't have to remember what you said yesterday to avoid contradicting yourself today. Your critics may call you every name in the book, but they can never accurately use the name *liar.* And a number of people, in their heart of hearts, will wish they had the courage to speak the truth as sincerely as you do.

The ancient Greeks are the ones who gave us the term "sincere." It means "without wax." It was common in those days for unscrupulous sculptors to cover over a defect in the marble with clear wax. To the untrained eye, this deception was hard to detect. So smart buyers would ask, "Is this sincere?" Then they would place the sculpture in the hot sun to see if it was. If the marble could stand the scrutiny of the sun without melting, it was "without wax."

The real benefit of living a life of candor is that you can stand the heat of examination and be proven a sincere person. And the people who really matter will respect you.

Rude Awakenings Are Still Rude

People sometimes confuse candor with rudeness, but the two are not synonymous. There is all the justification in the world for candor. There is none for rudeness, regardless of who you are or who you think you are. Sometimes rudeness comes from an elevated view of ourselves and our own station in life, like the rudeness a flight attendant experienced.

When the flight attendant offered a pillow to a woman in her airplane, the woman didn't answer. The attendant asked again. Still no reply. Then the woman's husband leaned over and said, "My wife doesn't talk to the help." His answer gave the reason for her rudeness, but that hardly excused it. And it hardly offered any consolation to the flight attendant.

I believe much rudeness stems from insensitivity, like the rudeness I experienced one day at the airport. Not long after my father died, Susan insisted I take a vacation to recuperate from the loss, and at the airport on the way home we ran into a man I had met in Christian circles.

"What are you doing here?" he asked.

"My father just passed away. We were taking a few days at a resort near here to recuperate."

"What resort?" he asked.

I told him the name.

"That place?" he smirked. "We used to stay there, too, but we weren't pleased with their service. Now we stay at—," and he named a very exclusive resort.

Not only did this man put down the place where we stayed, he never offered any expression of sympathy over my father's passing.

Insensitivity, though, doesn't account for all the world's rudeness. Some of it comes from a simple lack of manners.

After the 1992 election when the Democratic Party won the White House as well as a majority in both houses of Congress, Republican Senator Arlen Specter happened to step onto an elevator with an entertainer well-known for her support of Democratic candidates. "I guess we showed you guys, didn't we?" she taunted.

"I won," Specter replied quietly. Throwing defeat into the face of an opponent is hardly good manners, either.

Contrast that lack of manners with my experience in Romania years before communism fell. On more than one occasion I was hosted by Romanian Christians who lived well below the poverty line. Yet each time we sat down to eat, they offered a large meal. Their intent was to treat me as an honored guest. Only later did I learn that the family had given me all they had, forcing them to go without food for several days after I left.

Unlike rudeness, candor is the honest, loving, sensitive, and discreet presentation of truth. It is always polite, gracious, and courteous. It respects the dignity and feelings of other people. It says things so clearly that people cannot mistake what is meant. It won't allow a *no* to sound like a *yes.*

That's not to say that candor is always pleasant. The truth sometimes hurts. But rudeness is needless offense, while candor is an act of love and friendship that always contains a redemptive purpose. Solomon observed, "Better is open rebuke than hidden love," and "Wounds from a friend can be trusted, but an enemy multiplies kisses" (Proverbs 27:5,6).

For the kiss of candor to be most effective, a relationship must already exist. People need to sense we care for them before we confront them. Before we speak, we need to have won the right to be heard. In short, the more that people like us, the more they will listen to us.

I remember two friends approaching me while I was in seminary and saying, "John, every time we plan something, you have to be in control." Their rebuke stung, but because of the time and effort they had already invested in our friendship, they had earned the right to speak.

As much as that confrontation hurt, it wasn't nearly as painful as the time I was led to believe I had done a good job when, in fact, I hadn't. Early in my ministry, I conducted a church leadership seminar in another part of the country. As a young pastor, I felt insecure about the opportunity, so I invited a friend of mine from the area, whom I'll call Kent, to sit in on my session. He was an expert in church leadership, so I asked him to listen and offer his honest critique.

I knew I had much to learn, and I wanted to grow from the experience. So after the seminar, I took him to a local restaurant, and once we were seated and handed menus, I looked over at Kent and said, "Tell me how I can improve on my seminar."

"You were terrific," he smiled. "Absolutely terrific. In fact, I think you may be too big for the local church. We ought to get you on the national circuit."

I was elated, swelling with pride on the inside and smiling ear to ear. I respected this man's opinion. That made the compliment all the more valuable.

Sometime later, though, the smile went away. I was talking on the phone to another friend who lives in the same area. "John, I was just with Kent the other day," he said.

"Really? He sat in on my seminar. He told me he really liked it."

There was a pause. "Uh, he told me it was juvenile," my friend said.

I wasn't so much offended by Kent's criticism as by his deception. I asked for the truth. He gave me a lie. And in lying to me, he dishonored me, missing an opportunity to help me grow. And I missed the growth. In the moment of truth, the currency of his opinions, which I had treasured so highly, suddenly became devalued. So did my opinion of him.

Because this person wouldn't risk being candid, he risked something else.

His character.

And where do you go to retrieve that—or to get it if you've never had it?

CAPTAINS COURAGEOUS AND COMPASSIONATE

The courage of candor must always be balanced with compassion. Too often, we focus on the courageous aspect. "Did it ever take guts to say that in front of everyone." It *does* take guts. It also takes heart. And we should focus on the compassion that's needed when we tell the truth to someone who desperately needs to hear it.

Some of the people most desperate for truth are alcoholics. Often the most difficult step in reaching an alcoholic is the intervention. That's when friends and family sit down with the alcoholic to explain how that person's drinking is affecting them. If no one loves the alcoholic enough to do that, chances are the addiction will end up killing him. In this case, telling the truth is a life or death decision. If your courage can't come through to help you make that decision to confront, maybe your compassion for the person will. That's how the two work in tandem.

To speak candidly also takes faith. If it is the right thing to say, we must have faith that God will help us say it. Let me urge caution at this point. We need to take our time, listen to others, and test our motivation before we go charging off to say something difficult. We need to ask the questions, "Is this the right thing to say?" "Is this the right time to say it?" "Am I the right person to say it?"

Once we feel we have answered those questions, we can trust God for the strength to be candid. We can also trust Him for the results. When I was in campus ministry, we encouraged students to witness in the power of the Spirit, then leave the results to God. The same principle is true when showing candor.

Just as the seed can fall by the wayside and not penetrate the soil, so candor can fall on hearts not prepared to receive it. In that case, there is no growth. A consultant friend of mine learned the hard truth of that parable when he was invited to evaluate the effectiveness of a parachurch ministry project. He spent time studying the work, interviewing staff members, and gathering data. Finally, he presented his candid critique. He reported that while the project had good intentions, it was failing to meet its objectives. He later learned that when he left the room, the team members ridiculed his comments. They decided he was misinformed and judgmental, and they rejected his evaluation. Five years later, the director of the ministry project recommended it be shut down. It simply wasn't meeting its goals. If they had been willing to deal with the critique the consultant had offered years earlier, that ministry might be active today. Instead of receiving the words he so honestly and faithfully had given, they rejected them. And in rejecting them, the opportunity for growth was snatched away.

When our candor is balanced with courage and compassion, it's not up to us to worry about the response to our candor. Truth eventually wins out, even if it takes a long time to do so. When we're speaking honestly and with integrity, we can leave the results to God.

Again, a caution is needed. We must be certain of our motivation. Is it to speak the truth in love? Or is it to tell someone off? Are we using the truth as a scalpel to do surgery or as a steak knife to stab someone in the back? The only way we can understand our motivations is to move slowly, talk to trusted counselors, pray about it, and be ruthlessly honest with ourselves.

That said, we can't let concerns about our reputation, staying in the good graces of the system, or protecting ourselves from being attacked keep us from speaking out. Courage always involves an element of risk.

When I was living in Minnesota, I was faced with such a risk in my relationship with my dentist. He had sent me to a specialist, which turned out to be a disappointing experience. The specialist's personal hygiene wasn't good. His office wasn't clean. I even wondered if his instruments were properly sterilized. Since my longtime dentist friend had referred me to the specialist, I faced a dilemma: Should I risk telling my dentist that his referral was substandard?

On my next visit to my dentist I said, "I've been coming to you for seventeen years. I appreciate you. You embody my standard for professionalism. But I expect the same standard of care from your specialist as I do from you, and the one you referred me to didn't meet those expectations." I went on to share my concerns.

"John, if faithful patients like you don't tell me the truth," my friend replied, "who will?"

The next time I came in he said, "John, I've had two more complaints since you visited that specialist. I'm not referring to him again."[4]

THE OPPOSITE OF CANDOR

We tend to believe that the flip side of candor is sensitivity, that using candor is at one end of the spectrum and being tender toward people's feelings is at the other. Yet as we've already discussed, sensitivity to the person we are talking with is essential to being candid. Without that sensitivity, our candor becomes a wrecking ball. Instead of telling the truth in love, we treat the other person with disrespect.

The true opposite of candor is cowardice. Let me demonstrate this by using an example from real life with events and names changed to protect the guilty. I call this "The Anatomy of a Critic."

Let's say Jack sits in on a Sunday school class and decides he doesn't like the way Jim teaches it. So he goes to the education pastor, Jill, and complains about the lesson's content and Jim's competency.

Jill later calls up Jim and tells him about Jack's criticisms. The next Sunday, Jim approaches Jack and says, "I hear you have some concerns about the class I'm teaching."

Jack's face turns red, and he says, "Who told you that?"

"Why, Jill did."

"She had no right to do that," Jack yells and storms away.

That afternoon Jill gets a blistering phone call from Jack: "Who gave you permission to tell Jim what I said? You violated my confidence!"

"But Jack, the person who needed to hear this is not me but Jim. I'm not in that class. Jim can't improve unless you're honest with him."

"I was a fool for trusting you," replies Jack, slamming down the phone.

The problem in this scenario was not Jim's teaching skills. Nor was it Jill's decision to call Jim and share Jack's criticisms about him. The basic problem here is Jack's cowardice. He failed to show the commitment and courage to share his opinions with the person who needed—and deserved—to hear them.

Jack's actions were those of a sniper. He wanted to fire off his criticisms, camouflaged by anonymity. Without being seen. Without being shot at in return. Without helping Jim grow. And without being held accountable for the casualties.

Seems like a cowardly way to express your criticisms, doesn't it? And this is the opposite of how candor would express them.

BECOMING MORE MATURE

Not only do we need to learn how to be candid, but we must learn how to receive candor as well. That's one reason I respect Bill Hybels, pastor of Willow Creek Community Church. While pastoring a church of thousands has its benefits, it also exposes him to candid critiques from a large number of people.

Listen to how he has matured in his ability to receive criticism from others:

> In my early years of ministry, I rebutted people who wrote to me and said that I had offended them or hurt their feelings. For years I'd write back and essentially say, "I'm sorry you took it wrong, but there really wasn't anything wrong with what I said." But then they'd write back, doubly hurt. They knew what I really meant was, "I'm sorry you're so sensitive about petty things."
>
> After several years of doing this, I thought, What if I just said, "Thank you for writing me and expressing your hurt. I'm sorry. I didn't intend to hurt you. Please forgive me."
>
> Soon after implementing this approach, I began receiving letters saying, "Thank you for your letter. You don't know how much it means to me."

Many people, I discovered, just want to know if their pastor is a safe person. Can he respond to hurt with compassion? Does he care as much about relationships as sermon material? Our people already know we make mistakes. What they want to know is whether or not we have the integrity to admit them.[5]

It takes more than integrity to admit mistakes. It takes maturity. And one essential element of maturity is taking some measure of responsibility for our words and actions.

When I say, "You've grossly misunderstood me," I put the entire blame on you for any misunderstanding. How much better to say, "Perhaps I said this wrong" or "Maybe I'm not communicating very well."

Our goal ought to be to become more mature, not simply older. Learning to give and receive candor in a gracious manner is a crucial part of that process.

CHAPTER 5

MERCY

IN ARIZONA, WHERE I LIVE, I SEE A LOT OF BLUE HAIR AMONG the senior set. I'm amazed that older people with blue hair can be so critical of younger people with, say, green or orange hair. I mentioned this while preaching at a church in Washington where a young man with green hair was attending.

When he heard my comment, he said to himself, *Maybe I can be accepted here. Maybe this place is the real thing.* In his case—and I am not suggesting this is true in every case—he colored his hair green to express his anger and his sense of isolation over his wife leaving him because of his drug abuse.

The people at this church accepted the man, green hair and all. They helped lead him to Christ, helped him get off drugs, and helped him reconcile with his family. The key word here is "helped." He needed it. They gave it. They gave it because they were able to look beyond appearances to see the man's needs.

THE IMPORTANCE OF MERCY

Mercy is important if we are going to help people overcome the hurts of their past. Pain from the past has a way of burrowing under the surface of our lives and staying there. Unless dealt with, the pain has a way of worming around inside us, eating away at vital parts of our soul. When someone touches a sensitive place where the pain has burrowed, we react. The reaction may be a subtle flinch, a verbal slap on the hand, or a shove. Our words may be harsh and cruel, our behavior rude and offensive. It is often difficult to see past the reaction, but beyond it lies sensitive inner tissue, tender from the inflammation of past hurts.

For example, a friend of mine who is in high-level management had a boss who was absolutely profane, disrespectful, and crude to everyone he worked with. When my friend approached him about his behavior, the man denied it. One day my friend talked with a close friend of his who was one of the company's vendors. The vendor told him that the boss had a reputation for being an unreasonable customer. His language was always disrespectful and profane. He constantly complained that prices were too high and that the packaging was faulty. On top of all that, he demanded at least a 15 percent discount. The vendor said his company simply boosted its prices by 15 percent, then negotiated down to placate the man.

That's what people saw on the surface. Beneath the surface was another story. Later, my friend discovered that this man's family virtually ignored him. Maybe he deserved it, who knows? But maybe the pain of that isolation—which he carries inside to every meeting, every appointment, every negotiation—eats away at his insides in a way that none of us can see or understand, prompting him to act badly toward others.

Almost everybody lives with some degree of hidden pain. My father, for example, was a battered child from an impoverished family. He carried that pain within him for years. Although you would never have known it, that child still lived inside the man he grew up to become.

He was the oldest of eleven children from a family that lived "on the other side of the tracks" in Grand Junction, Colorado. When his high-school class celebrated its fortieth reunion at the Grand Junction country club, he decided to go. As my parents drove their new luxury car through the front gate, memories of my father's childhood clamored in his mind. He had worked at that country club as a young boy trying to survive. There, the contrast between the "haves" and the "have-nots" was inescapable. Even though the poor little boy he once was had grown up and become a successful businessman, the stigma of being so poor persisted in his memory long after he had achieved financial success. Entering those gates was almost a rite of passage for him, a threshold experience. In His own quiet way, the Holy Spirit transformed that experience into a visual symbol of my father putting the pain of his past behind him.

The pain of childhood, the pain of being fired, the pain of being rejected—there are countless hurts that can live within us long after the scars on the surface have healed. If we judge others by their coarse words and harsh reactions without looking beneath the surface to the wounds in the soul, we won't be following the example of the Great Physician Himself. And whatever treatment we will be able to give will only be topical, treating the symptoms but never the cause.

If we truly care about people, though, we will want to go beneath the surface to understand them and to extend mercy. That's what friends do. When I was in campus ministry, I got a call from a childhood friend, Scott Crawford. Scott told me his dad had died and asked me to conduct the funeral. At first I declined. I didn't want to do it. I wasn't even a pastor. But Scott persisted.

As I thought about what to say at the funeral, I realized that when Scott and I were boys, Mr. Crawford had always treated us as though we were men. He asked our opinions on political issues and listened to our answers. He never put us down for our adolescent opinions, rambling as they were. He never even cut those ramblings short. He treated us with merciful dignity. He helped us mature by listening to us and honoring us. By extending to us the uncommon grace of treating us like men, Mr. Crawford helped us *become* men.

I'm a better man because of him. I never realized it, though, until I took the time to look beneath the surface. And I built my eulogy around my view of Mr. Crawford as a merciful man.

Why Mercy Is Uncommon

As important as mercy is, it isn't common. Why is this?

One reason for the scarceness of mercy is selfishness. Selfishness is a characteristically adolescent way of viewing the universe and our place within it. One wit put it this way: "Galileo was wrong; the world does not revolve around the sun; it revolves around your teenage daughter." Do you remember being an adolescent? They tend to think only of themselves, not of others, confident that everything they believe is true, that everything they do is right. Hopefully, we grew up and went through a paradigm shift, learning to respect and care for others.

Not all of us who have grown up, though, have grown out of all aspects of our selfishness. Some adults may achieve great things, make huge amounts of money, and employ hundreds, even thousands of people. But they don't really care for those people. And the people around them know it.

This lack of concern is often evident even in the relationships that should be of the most concern to us—those within our own family. This is often most evident in rest homes. The old people there are lonely. Why? Their children don't call, don't write, don't drop by to visit, don't take them places. Why don't they? Because in many cases, the children are simply treating the parents the way the parents treated them when they were kids. The selfishness of the parents has been passed down to their children, just as surely as their DNA has been.

Often, though, selfishness isn't so obvious. A friend told

me about a man in a volunteer organization who was complaining about the president. My friend confronted the man on his attitude and said he owed it to the president to speak to him about his concerns. The response was, "I'll tell him when he's on his way out the door."

This man acted as judge and jury of the organization's president, but he was not willing to accept the responsibility of telling him the verdict. That's judgment, not mercy. Selfishness, not servanthood. He was not serving the president, the organization, or even himself. And he certainly wasn't serving Christ.

A second reason mercy is uncommon is that some individuals are project-oriented rather than people-oriented. Some people are so focused on the work that needs to be done that everything else blurs into the background, including individuals' needs.

A friend told me about walking through the warehouse of a large Christian organization with its owner, who didn't acknowledge a single employee. It was as though the employees were machines rather than human beings. Most businesses are busy places; I understand that. I also understand that Jesus, whose partnership with His Father was a twenty-four-hour-a-day job, was never too busy for a single person. Never.

Lack of acknowledgment is a subtle form of corporate abuse. Such treatment has long-term consequences. In a book review of *Corporate Abuse: How "Lean and Mean" Robs People and Profits* by Lesley Wright and Marti Smye, *Chicago Tribune* staff writer Chuck Hutchcraft wrote that acceptance is

> a major problem in an abusive work environment. Pretty soon, we come to accept abuse as though it is part of the job. We get on with it. But it has its costs. Big costs. Personal costs, in terms of our health, productivity, creativity, our careers, our very souls. And in the long run it is shortsighted and ends up costing the company too.[1]

In contrast to the darkness that selfishness and insensitivity bring with them, mercy walks into a room and brightens everything. A friend of mine came into such a room as a guest at a country club, and immediately his eye caught a Hispanic worker who seemed dejected. He was surrounded by country club members, yet he was being totally ignored. My friend remembers about forty Spanish words from his high school Spanish class, but he greeted the worker with the few he knew. The worker jerked his head up, breaking out in a huge smile and a torrent of Spanish words that my friend couldn't keep up with. My friend was simply trying to show mercy to lift the worker's spirits. Who would have thought such a small gesture would have made such an impact?

A third reason we withhold mercy is because we have not resolved past hurts. Survival is a strong and necessary instinct that sometimes causes us to perceive other people as enemies. Frankly, there are some people who *are* enemies, and we *should* protect ourselves from them. However, those people are the exception. The rule is that most people who have hurt us are not our enemies. They may have offended us. They may have told us off. They may have talked behind our backs. But mercy has the power to break that cycle, both in them and in our response to them. If we withhold mercy, though, those people will continue to have a negative hold on us. And if we withhold mercy, then we will always be focused on ourselves instead of on the needs to be met in the lives of other people.

A counselor told me of a person who years ago had a disagreement with a colleague that was filled with harsh words punctuated by sweeping accusations. Later the colleague apologized. The first party listened to the apology but said nothing about his own words and accusations, which were just as harsh, just as sweeping. Afterward, the relationship continued as it had before. All was well, or so it seemed. But the person who withheld the mercy of his own apology still talks about that day when he was maligned and hurt. For all the appearance of the relationship being restored, it wasn't. Look beneath appearances, and see if you don't agree.

- Whatever the man may have said, he hasn't forgiven his colleague. If he had forgiven him, he wouldn't continue to bring up the incident.
- The man has refused to accept responsibility for his actions. Only one of them confessed and repented, yet both behaved improperly.
- The man doesn't really care about his colleague. If he did, he wouldn't malign him in front of other people. Instead, he would do and say things that would build up the relationship instead of tearing it down.

Sadly, these responses are not unusual. While anger is a normal response to pain or injustice and is an emotion God Himself experiences, nurturing that anger leads to sin. Nurturing that anger also prevents us from manifesting mercy. Left to itself, anger breaks down into bitterness and resentment to form the compost out of which grows vengeance—in our minds if not in our actions. And mercy, which so wonderfully feeds our own souls, is nowhere to be found.

We all know people who can't manifest mercy and get on with life because they have never resolved a hurt from their past. What was once a fresh wound is now a festering sore. The writer of Hebrews warned, "See to it that no one misses the grace of God and that no bitter root grows up to cause trouble and defile many" (12:15). The root of the word "bitter" alludes to a sharp stick that can seriously injure you if you are jabbed with it. That's what bitter people do—a lot of jabbing. They may use a sharp stick to do it, or simply a toothpick. It doesn't really matter. Even a toothpick can do a lot of damage if poked into the right place or if poked deeply enough or often enough.

One of the most obvious ways in which this "poking" happens is when the embittered person strikes back at the one who caused the problem to begin with. The embittered person may provoke an angry confrontation or may simply withhold certain social courtesies, such as not making eye contact or not smiling when eye contact is made.

A second way in which a bitter person retaliates is less direct. The injured party may fight back by saying harmful things behind the offender's back. Anything that will destroy the person's reputation is considered fair game. Anything that will lower the respect others have for the offender is considered legitimate. "All's fair in love and war" is the embittered person's motto. And make no mistake: The embittered person *is* at war.

Probably the most bitter person I ever knew was a man I'll call Joe. He had been hurt by some serious sins his wife had committed. Even though she was genuinely sorry and apologetic, he was unforgiving. As a result, he slowly sank into a bog of bitterness. If a man said something nice about his own wife, Joe criticized women in general. If a friend had a great relationship with his own wife, Joe found something negative to say about it.

The day came when some friends decided to confront Joe about his behavior. These people were genuine friends—they loved him and cared for him. And they paid a price for confronting him, for rather than listening to them, Joe turned on them.

A "bitter root grows up to cause trouble and defile many," said the writer of Hebrews. That's why he was so emphatic that the "bitter root" be removed. Because like Joe's bitterness, it never stays a root. It grows like a thorny vine, and whoever gets too close gets pricked.

How We Show Mercy

The healthiest people are those who extend mercy. Their motivation is not personal aggrandizement or professional advancement. They are not motivated by self. They are captivated by others. Their concern for other people manifests itself in acts of mercy. The acts are as varied as each individual need calls for. In one instance, mercy could take the form of an employer confronting an employee to avert an otherwise inevitable firing. In another case, mercy could take the form of catching a friend in a lie and encouraging the person to own up to it. Mercy does have its hard side. And depending on the situation, that hard side should be shown. But mercy has a soft side, too, and that should also be shown, especially with those less fortunate.

I am making a new friend in Phoenix who has a ministry to the less fortunate, to children of ex-convicts and drug addicts. In many cases these kids have had little supervision. My friend tells of taking a boy to a restaurant for breakfast, where the boy ordered a stack of pancakes. When the food arrived, he stabbed the top three pancakes with his fork, held them in front of his mouth, and started to tear into them.

No one had ever told this young man about appropriate and inappropriate table manners. And where he has lived, if you don't grab the food and eat it fast, you go hungry. My friend understood this, so he calmly corrected the boy by explaining appropriate table manners. Those words of instruction were one of the first acts of mercy the young man had ever received. By learning acceptable public behavior, he stands a better chance of succeeding in the workplace and avoiding the problems his parents have faced.

It is important not to confuse mercy with sympathy. It is not a feeling but an action. It moves. It motivates. It makes a difference in people's lives. But to make that difference, mercy sometimes has to be blunt. I have a friend who privately confronted an older colleague at work with these words: "Gerald [not his real name], everyone thinks you act like an old goat." My friend wasn't trying to be rude or disrespectful. He simply recognized from past experience that the older man was oblivious to how his behavior was affecting other people. The proverbial two-by-four over the head was ineffective. He needed to be hit by a tree.

The "old goat" description was that tree. The older man finally recognized what he was doing and changed. Relationships with other employees were transformed, and the company flourished.

Obviously, we shouldn't use a tree when a two-by-four will do. And we shouldn't use a two-by-four when some gentler form of communication will do, like the one Roy Jones used. Roy was a member of the church I pastored in Minneapolis. At the time, the church was getting some rough treatment at the hands of the city council over a building project. (Parenthetically, my friend David Davenport was mayor then. This was before our friendship began. I still tell him the city [translation: mayor] was wrong. He just laughs at me.) Of course, none of us was laughing then. In fact, I got pretty angry about it—so much so that my anger spilled over into a sermon. What I said was out of line—hardly my finest hour in the pulpit. That week Roy wrote me a thoughtful letter about how much my sermons had touched him, and how he appreciated my leadership, but how I was a much better person than my behavior during that moment in the sermon had demonstrated. Instead of scolding me, he affirmed me. Instead of telling me I was a jerk, he complimented me. He showed me mercy rather than attacking me, and his words helped me become not only a better pastor but a better person.

> He could have used a tree.
> He could have used a two-by-four.
> Instead, all he used were a sheet of paper and
> a few kind words.

THE COST OF MERCY

It is not always easy to show mercy. It is difficult to let go of the hurt that people have inflicted in the past or to extend mercy to someone who presents some real threat to us. Part of the difficulty comes when we think that showing mercy means eliminating justice. While justice and mercy are different, they aren't necessarily mutually exclusive. A desire for justice, for example, cannot be used as a defense for refusing to show mercy. Jesus told us that the more important matters of the law include both justice and mercy (Matthew 23:23). The difference between the two is this: Justice seeks responsibility for the offense, while mercy seeks restoration for the offender.

If that's not clear, maybe this example will help. A few years ago our daughter, Stephanie, was living in Seattle. One night while she was walking from the store to her downtown apartment, a man jumped her from behind. She was so frightened she couldn't even scream, but fortunately something startled her attacker, and he ran away.

As soon as Stephanie got home, she called us. When I heard about her terrifying experience, I was ready to take the first plane to Seattle. What I wanted to do was drive Stephanie through the streets, looking for her attacker. If she spotted him, I would jump out of the car, hold him until the police arrived, and see him put in prison. That is justice.

While mercy would not have ignored the crime, it would have gone one step further. Justice would hold the man accountable for his actions, but mercy would hold out an opportunity for change. Justice would sit in the courtroom long enough to hear the verdict, then walk away. Mercy would stay after the sentencing to try to figure out how to get him the psychological and spiritual help he needed to start a better life so that once he was released, he wouldn't repeat his offenses.

Extending mercy to someone who has wronged us does not mean we take the dead bolts off our door. We still need to take precautions. It would be criminal, for example, to allow a pedophile unsupervised time with children in the name of mercy. Sometimes because of the danger a person presents, we need to show mercy indirectly. In such circumstances it

might be safer to have a third party involved. By having someone else intervene, mercy can be extended without taking
unnecessary risks.

However it is accomplished, we must be willing to con-
tribute to the growth of those around us rather than cling to a
desire for revenge. Jesus made it abundantly clear that forgiveness is not some alternative therapy with a high success
rate in dealing with victimization. Forgiveness is not an alternative but an imperative. And the ramifications of our response
to that imperative are far-reaching, touching the very throne
where justice and mercy originate. At the end of the Lord's
Prayer, Jesus said, "For if you forgive men when they sin
against you, your heavenly Father will also forgive you. But if
you do not forgive men their sins, your Father will not forgive
your sins" (Matthew 6:14-15). Pretty sobering words, especially
for the victims.

A young man in a church I pastored was himself a victim
who was verbally and emotionally abused by his father.
Recently I heard a sermon that this young man preached on
forgiveness. He said he realized that the hatred he felt toward
his father was wrong, so he asked to have lunch with him. He
told his father he had hated him for his actions, but then he
realized that as a follower of Christ, he was wrong to hold onto
that hatred. He asked his father to forgive him, not only for the
hatred but for all the hateful things he had ever said to him.
Until that moment, the young man's father had never admitted that any of his behavior was wrong. But after forgiving his
son, the father asked forgiveness, too. He admitted his abusive
words and actions, and he apologized. The son's merciful
step—even though he had been the victim—led not only to
healing his wounds but to restoring the relationship.

It is important to distinguish between releasing someone
from the debt of what he has done to you and reconciling a
relationship. The young man forgave his father and asked forgiveness for his hatred. But it was only after the father repented

of his wrongdoing that they were able to reconcile and begin to rebuild their relationship.

In some situations, reconciliation simply will not happen. Dr. Darryl DelHousaye, senior pastor of Scottsdale Bible Church and my successor as president of Phoenix Seminary, says that more than once he has had two people sit in his office and swear that they did not say what the other person was accusing them of. Neither individual will admit that he did anything wrong. There is always the "Six Men from Indostan" principle at work: each man is blind and describes the part of an elephant he can touch, therefore perceiving and revealing something different about the truth of an elephant. But we all know of situations where problems exist not because of differing perspectives, but because individuals refuse to accept responsibility for their actions.

How do you reconcile with someone who will not own up to his wrongdoing? The Bible tells us that sometimes there will be no resolution. Romans 12:18 says, "If it is possible, as far as it depends on you, live at peace with everyone." Sadly, there are some people who can never admit their fault in a dispute. It is impossible to be at peace with such people. All we can do is put forth our best effort at peace, then walk away if it is rejected.

Extending mercy doesn't always bring peace. Even when it does, the peace process is seldom easy. It's not easy letting go of past hurts. It's not easy asking forgiveness. And it's not easy extending it. It takes time and energy. And it often takes a toll on us, emotionally, spiritually, and physically. But the toll is part of the cost of following Christ, a toll He Himself paid. In Matthew 20:28, Jesus said that He "did not come to be served, but to serve." And He said in John 15:13, "Greater love has no one than this, that he lay down his life for his friends." It takes a selfless person to follow that example. So much of the time, though, we're so self-absorbed that we can't even *see* the needs of others, let alone meet them.

THE BENEFITS OF MERCY

While extending mercy comes at a price, failure to do so exacts a higher price. Dr. Paul Carlson says that studies of retired residents living in the well-known retirement community of Sun City, Arizona, show that the people who retire and serve others stay healthier longer, while the ones who serve only themselves quickly atrophy.

Extending mercy not only helps us retain our physical health but our psychological health as well. I'm thinking of a young woman who suffered painful ridicule when she was in school. When she graduated, she thought the pain of those years was behind her. But it wasn't. Eventually she realized she needed to deal with those memories. One by one, she contemplated the people whose words had been so hurtful to her. And one by one, she forgave them. It was an intensely personal, private time, but her acts of forgiveness freed her from those painful words.

Later, one of her classmates told the young woman's brother that his internal struggles had motivated him to look for targets on whom he could release all the anger inside him. That young woman was an easy target. When she learned of her classmate's admission, she was able to respond with understanding rather than vengeance. When mercy triumphs like that, there are no losers. Everybody wins.

There are some relationships, though, that have no chance for reconciliation. I'm talking about a relationship with someone who has died. How can we free ourselves from old wounds when the one who has wounded us is gone? My father faced that dilemma. While he never told me he hated his father, he would say things like, "I hope your brother and you respect me more than I respect *my* father." After my grandfather's funeral, my father's only comment was, "I am sad that I am not sad."

My father's life as the oldest of eleven kids was painful. As a child, he was battered. As a teenager, he fought back. He and the next-oldest son threatened my grandfather. They told him if he didn't stop beating the younger kids the way he had beaten them, they'd kill him.

My father died fairly suddenly from a brain tumor. Afterward, his pastor told me of a time when the two of them were driving to a conference with a counselor who was to be the speaker. Somehow they got to talking about my grandfather, and my father confessed how much he hated him, even though he was already dead. My father admitted, "I do not know how to get over the hatred I feel toward someone who is dead." The counselor very wisely answered, "Your father may be dead, but Jesus is alive. If you will give your hatred to Jesus, He will deal with it however He deals with hatred toward dead people." They pulled off the freeway, and my father prayed a prayer that went something like this: "Jesus, I hate my father. He is dead. You are alive. So I give You my hatred toward my father and ask You to deal with it however You will."

My father was never one to drop by anywhere unexpectedly, but a few days later he burst into his pastor's office unannounced and said, "For the first time in my life I am free of the hatred I felt toward my father."

I've talked about many concepts in this chapter: Letting go of the past. Showing mercy. Serving others. And I've used a lot of examples to illustrate them. But there is no better example than Jesus Himself. When He was being crucified, Jesus prayed, "Father, forgive them, for they do not know what they are doing" (Luke 23:34). Reflecting on that example, the apostle Peter said this:

> But how is it to your credit if you receive a beating for doing wrong and endure it? But if you suffer for doing good and you endure it, this is commendable before God. To this you were called, because Christ suffered for you, leaving you an example, that you should follow in his steps. "He committed no sin,

and no deceit was found in his mouth." When they hurled their insults at him, he did not retaliate; when he suffered, he made no threats. Instead, he entrusted himself to him who judges justly. (1 Peter 2:20-23)

Maybe the most appropriate way to end this chapter is to share what the writer of Hebrews suggests we do. "Consider him who endured such opposition from sinful men, so that you will not grow weary and lose heart" (12:3).

CHAPTER 6

KINDNESS

I WAS FLYING HOME FROM TENNESSEE, READING THE NASHVILLE paper, when the photograph of a young woman in her early twenties caught my eye. The reason it did was that the woman's face didn't have a nose. Instead she had something that looked like a metal plate. As I looked closer, her eyes looked unusual, too. I couldn't tell if they were focused on the camera taking her photograph, but they looked fixed and vacant. *A hideous picture to put in a public newspaper.* That was my first thought.

Until I read the story.

Twenty-two years ago, this young woman was born without a face. There were tiny slits almost at the sides of her head instead of eye sockets. She was blind. She had no nose or palate, just two small holes. Her parents were so overcome with grief that they couldn't keep her, so a social worker and her husband adopted her. The newspaper interviewed both the young woman and her adoptive mother. The occasion was the daughter's graduation from a special program in college that was tailored for disabled students. The adoptive mother told the reporter, "This has been the greatest experience of my life."

Contrast that woman with a woman on the very same flight. I don't know her. I've never spoken one word to her or heard one from her. But I know this: I don't like her. I don't like her because she would not quit staring at a passenger who had growths covering his face. The growths were unattractive, but not as unattractive as her behavior. I wasn't the only person on the plane who noticed it. She made the flight awkward for everyone, and, in the process, embarrassed not only the man but herself. A baby without a face was cherished by a woman who understood something beyond appearances. A man *with* a face was embarrassed by another woman who understood nothing *but* appearances. What did the one understand that the other didn't?

WHAT IS KINDNESS?

The difference between the two women was that the first one understood kindness to its fullest extent. The other one didn't. The fragrance of that woman's kindness was so pure and so sweet, almost like the smell of some lush, tropical fruit. Kindness is in fact a fruit, a fruit that the Holy Spirit produces in a Christian's life (Galatians 5:22-23).

But what is it exactly?

Kindness is an attitude of graciousness, a generosity of heart. But it doesn't stop there; it leads to *acts* of kindness. Kindness won't let me stand back and watch you in some kind of trouble and just think sympathetic thoughts about you. Kindness doesn't allow me simply to make a prayerful wish that God bring someone into your life to meet those needs. I must *be* that someone. The kindness *inside* requires expression *outside*.

The word "kindness" listed in Galatians 5 has the sense of being faithful to an obligation made to a friend or relative. The Greek word used there is the same word used in the Septuagint, the Greek translation of the Old Testament, to describe the good that we receive because of God's faithful commitment to His people. "Lovingkindness" is the way it's most often translated. When we show kindness to others, we demonstrate the faithfulness of our love to them. It's a sign of the commitment we have to them, a sign of our loyalty to the relationship. As such, it is a reflection of the covenant relationship that God has with us. It is sobering to recognize that if we don't show kindness, then we are distorting that reflection—and therefore distorting the very image of the Almighty.

KINDNESS FACES TOUGH ISSUES

When we don't show kindness, it distorts our relationships with God and with others. We often think that the opposite of being kind is simply being mean-spirited and harsh, actively seeking someone's harm. That is partly true. But there are more subtle ways of being unkind.

If you grew up in a volatile family, you probably learned ways of responding that minimized conflict and kept you out of trouble. Being quiet and helpful might have been one of those ways. You may think of such a response as showing kindness. In fact, it is often just the opposite. Refusing to confront an abusive family member can be just as unkind as lashing out at him.

One of the most difficult responsibilities of a pastor is helping a family deal with the death of a teenager. That's why the crash of TWA flight 800 in the summer of 1996 affected me so deeply. I thought often about those high school kids from Pennsylvania who were on board for a trip with their French club. Our daughter, Stephanie, went on a trip like that when she was in school. I tried to imagine how the surviving families felt, but it was too painful to even try.

Then one day I was golfing with some acquaintances, and one woman asked, "Have you heard the jokes about the TWA crash?" I was stunned. I put my hands up and said, "Please don't tell them. There's too much pain associated with that crash. I've buried too many people. I've wept too much in funerals to hear those jokes."

Now, I could easily have rationalized away a need to say anything. I didn't know this person well. It wouldn't have hurt me to listen to the jokes. Besides, she might have thought I was making a big deal over nothing. But if I hadn't responded the way I did, this woman might inadvertently have told those jokes later on to someone who had lost a child through some other accident. Imagine the pain and embarrassment such a situation could cause. While it was a small decision to say that those jokes were not appropriate, it was kinder than letting this woman continue being insensitive to others.

The Bible reminds us that rebuke and correction can be expressions of kindness. David wrote in Psalm 141:5, "Let a righteous man strike me — it is a kindness; let him rebuke me — it is oil on my head. My head will not refuse it." David was not speaking theoretically. This was the same man who had committed adultery with Bathsheba and then had arranged for her husband to be murdered. Most people tiptoed around King David's sin. Maybe they didn't want to risk making him angry. Maybe they didn't want to jeopardize their jobs. Or their lives. Who knows for sure? But surely they all had their reasons.

Only one person stood up to David: the prophet Nathan. He cared enough not only to help David see what he had done but to recognize why it was so wrong. From that encounter, painful as it was, David learned something. He learned that when he needed correction, the kindest thing a person could do was to tell him the truth, not tiptoe around it.

I know of a Christian leader whose friend recently committed adultery and left her husband for another man. Although many of her friends tiptoed around the sin, this Christian leader didn't. She went to the woman and said, "We have been friends. I bring you a gift of love, but I also want you to know that I feel as though you have cheated on our relationship because you have lied to me."

The friend responded by saying, "Thank you so much for being honest and for sharing your convictions and your feelings, because I'm hearing through a third party that a number of my other Christian friends feel the same way but won't tell me." This leader has remained true to her convictions, but she has also opened the door for her friend to come to her for help if she changes her mind and wants to reestablish the relationships with her husband and children.

In the name of kindness we often ignore such problems to avoid a confrontation. Or we talk about the problem, but behind a person's back rather than to her face. It's easier that way. And safer. But true kindness, the kindness that reflects our loyalty to God, doesn't look for the easy way around a problem. And it doesn't look for the expedient way. It looks for the *right* way.

KINDNESS IS CONSISTENT

I recently heard from a friend of my son's, whom I've known since they were in kindergarten. A grown man now, he is successful in his career as a salesman. In spite of his success, he is constantly maligned by his boss—but always in private. The other employees in the company see the boss as funny, considerate, and sensitive. But my son's friend finds him demeaning, humiliating, and cruel. Why the contrast? Why two separate behaviors?

The apostle James described this inconsistency best when he wrote: "With the tongue we praise our Lord and Father, and with it we curse men, who have been made in God's likeness. Out of the same mouth come praise and cursing. My brothers, this should not be" (James 3:9-10).

We expect to see such inconsistencies from those who are ruled by their passions but not from those who say they are ruled by Christ. Yet I know a case of a well-respected public leader who has sexually abused his daughter in private. How could a person live such an inconsistent life, his public life all praise, his private life a curse? I don't know. I can only say with James, "My brothers, this should not be."

We should be consistent. We shouldn't act one way in public and another way in private. We shouldn't show kindness to one group of people and withhold it from another. Praises and curses shouldn't come from the same tongue.

Christ certainly expects consistency from us. He commanded us to "love your enemies, do good to them, and lend to them without expecting to get anything back. Then your reward will be great, and you will be sons of the Most High, because he is kind to the ungrateful and wicked" (Luke 6:35). All too often, though, we are kind only to those people who have "earned" our kindness. Jesus, in this verse, tells us just the opposite. If we want to be like God, we have to be consistent in our kindness. And that means being kind even to our enemies.

It's easy to forget this command when your enemies are attacking you. In the heat of battle, all sorts of arrows start to fly, even when the battle is with other Christians. A group of Christian scholars was having a verbal skirmish about a controversial subject when one of the men became angry and talked disrespectfully to those who disagreed with him. Noticing the man's lack of kindness, another participant loved him enough to say, "I don't see the fruit of the Spirit being manifested in your life right now." The man snapped back, "We're not talking about the fruit of the Spirit. We're talking about *truth!*"

Defending the truth is a noble thing. But *obeying* the truth is nobler. As followers of Christ we are called to obey Scripture, all of it. We can't justify disobeying one biblical truth by saying we are defending some other one. No matter what truth this man was defending, God still expected him to show kindness to those with whom he disagreed. Even though his "enemies" were people with different views, the man was still called to "do good to them."

Contrast that man's behavior with the apostle Paul's words in Ephesians 4:31-32: "Get rid of all bitterness, rage and anger, brawling and slander, along with every form of malice. Be kind and compassionate to one another, forgiving each other, just as in Christ God forgave you." Not only are we to be kind to one another, we have to allow the Spirit of God to delete from our hearts any sense of anger, rage, or bitterness. The standard is clear. The standard is unarguable. The standard is unequivocal. God expects us to be men and women who express ourselves in kindness, regardless of the battle or what enemy is waging it.

Charles L. Allen says, "If we could read the secret history of our enemies, we should find in each man's life sorrow and suffering enough to disarm all hostility." He then quotes John Cogley who says, "Tolerance implies a respect for another person, not because the person is wrong, or even right, but because the person is human."[1] Jesus Christ calls us not only to be men and women of truth, but to be men and women of relationships as well—men and women who express our care for one another by how we treat one another.

"Everywhere I turn, it seems, I hear of Christians under attack—not from secular humanists or fundamentalist Muslims, but from fellow members of the Christian community," wrote Philip Yancey in *Christianity Today*. Charles Colson told Yancey that the ugliest mail he has ever received came from Christians. "Our brethren were far less charitable than the secular media during the days of Watergate," he said. "It is time for us to realize that differences need not lead to division," Yancey declared. "It is time for us to remember that Jesus named love, not theological or political correctness, as the identifying mark of Christians."[2]

Kindness Doesn't Camouflage Anger

In the church, we have been taught that anger is a sin. But seldom have we been taught what to do with our anger. Though the church is sometimes silent, the Bible isn't. The Bible has much to say about anger and what we are to do with it.

One thing it tells us is that not all anger is wrong. "In your anger do not sin," wrote the apostle Paul. "Do not let the sun go down while you are still angry" (Ephesians 4:26). Paul used two words for anger in this verse. The first word means a "deep-seated conviction" that something is wrong. It is something like "righteous indignation," which contains within it the idea of a controlled response. In contrast to that idea, when Paul warned us not to "let the sun go down while you are still angry," he used a word that describes an emotional flare-up, an explosion of anger, an uncontrolled reaction.

As a careful writer, Paul understood the nuances of anger. He also understood the nuances of our humanity. We get angry at different things, for different reasons, and to different degrees. But we all get angry. If we deny that, we deny our humanity. The issue should be how we deal with the anger. I was talking with a man about a friend of his who carries anger inside him like a bottle of nitroglycerin: The slightest disturbance, and it explodes. When I mentioned the concept of not letting the sun go down on our anger, the man rationalized his friend's sin by saying, "But the sun sets very slowly for my friend."

In my opinion, both men were wrong. The man who had not dealt with his anger was wrong. So was the friend who was unwilling to confront him. He rationalized it. He excused it. And, in the language of recovery programs, he "enabled" it. The man to whom I was talking finds himself constantly answering for his friend. By answering for him instead of holding him accountable, he is allowing a dysfunctional and sinful person to remain stuck. He never helps his friend work through his anger. And he never encourages others to help him, either. The reason for this is simple pragmatism—he doesn't think it will do any good.

These men are not unique. Too many people who have a relationship with the God of reconciliation live without reconciliation in their relationships with others. That is tragic, because anger is such a destructive emotion.

When Solomon wrote, "A hot-tempered man stirs up dissension" (Proverbs 15:18), he was telling us that anger rarely erupts without the emotional balance of all those around becoming unsettled. Because those eruptions can be so frightening, we've trained people to suppress their anger, to pretend it doesn't exist, to paste a smile on their face and go on with the program. The problem with this solution is that it doesn't work. Anger cannot be suppressed, not for long anyway. Eventually it will erupt, and everyone around will get burned.

Over the years, I've worked with a number of retired military personnel in ministry settings. At times some of them would be upset about something I asked them to do, but instead of acknowledging their feelings and resolving the conflict, they simply said, "Yes, sir!" Throughout their careers, they had been trained to give unquestioning obedience to their leaders, and because they perceived their pastor to be their leader, they responded to me in the same way. They said the right words, did the right things, but had the wrong attitude. Over time it affected them, which in turn affected the ministry they were trying to have in other people's lives.

When we suppress our anger, we may succeed in hiding it from the person with whom we disagree, but at some point it will surface elsewhere. I remember such an occurrence when I was speaking at a men's retreat in Arizona. The heat was sweltering, and there was no air conditioning, so we had all the doors and windows open. Suddenly, a group of high-school kids pulled onto the retreat grounds with their car radio blaring. One of the men, a retired high-school teacher, was visibly upset and shot out of his seat to shut the doors and the windows.

Immediately the room grew hot and stuffy, and we desperately needed air. Because of the size of the group, we had been able to talk quite openly with each other during the retreat. This man, in particular, had participated quite often, so I simply asked him if he was upset.

"Yes, I'm *very* upset," he responded. "Those kids don't have the right to disturb our meeting."

From the reactions of the other men, it was clear that the retired teacher was the only person who thought that the music was disturbing us. So I probed deeper. "Are those kids putting the anger into you, or are they just bringing it out?"

The more he tried to blame his anger on those kids, the more obvious it became that he had a backlog of anger. Those particular kids were not the source of it. The problem originated in him.

While suppressing anger may seem like a kind thing to do, it isn't. This doesn't mean we should vent our anger in an uncontrolled outburst. It does mean we should respond to tense situations with honest yet controlled emotions.

KINDNESS DRAWS PEOPLE TO CHRIST

Years ago when I was pastoring in Minneapolis, a World Vision representative came to the church to raise funds for famine victims in Africa. He showed the movie "Empty Bellies Have No Ears," which argues that if people are starving, they're not going to hear our words about Christ. That principle applies to our culture as well. People are hurting, people are frightened, people are without direction, and they are not going to hear our words about Jesus if we don't first attend to their other needs.

Sadly, kindness is in short supply for the very people who need it most—even in the church. I have a friend in the church who years ago asked his wife for a divorce. Today he recognizes that divorce is wrong, that God hates it, and he wishes he had never gotten one. But no matter how his views or heart have changed, he can't change the fact that he is divorced. He can't undo the mistakes he made.

Because of those mistakes, some of the people in the church refuse to talk to him or associate with him, even after many years. Understandably, he's hurt. "Is this what we are saying to society?" he asks. "'Do it exactly my way, or else I will isolate and ostracize you'?"

Both in the church and in society, people feel isolated and ostracized. Is it any wonder we are "cocooning" as a culture? We are increasingly becoming people who withdraw into a private world made up of our family and perhaps a few friends with whom we feel safe.

But the harshness that drives so many people into isolation also creates an opportunity. In this environment an act of kindness becomes a surprise, something that stands out. My wife, Susan, and I recently celebrated thirty years of marriage. As I told people we were getting ready to celebrate this milestone, I was surrounded by smiles, enthusiastic support, and expressions of great happiness for us. I'm convinced that I received this type of response because people recognize that not many couples today enjoy their marriages, and for those who do, there is no guarantee how long that enjoyment will last or even how long the relationship will last. The same is true of kindness. There is such a lack of kindness today that people take notice when they are treated kindly. If we desire to have an impact on people for Christ, we need to realize that we will only gain a hearing from them if we treat them with kindness.

Jesus repeatedly told His disciples to be kind to strangers. "If anyone gives even a cup of cold water to one of these little ones because he is my disciple, I tell you the truth, he will certainly not lose his reward," He said (Matthew 10:42). When He described a future judgment, Jesus said,

"Then the King will say to those on his right, 'Come,
you who are blessed by my Father; take your inheri-
tance, the kingdom prepared for you since the creation of the world. For I was hungry and you gave
me something to eat, I was thirsty and you gave me
something to drink, I was a stranger and you invited
me in, I needed clothes and you clothed me, I was
sick and you looked after me, I was in prison and
you came to visit me.' When someone asks, 'Lord,
when did we see you hungry and feed you, or thirsty
and give you something to drink?' the King replies,
'I tell you the truth, whatever you did for one of the
least of these brothers of mine, you did for me.'"
(Matthew 25:34-40)

There are many ways to hand a cup of cold water to a person. It can be a smile, a kind word, or holding a door open; it
can be offering to help carry a heavy suitcase in an airport. We
often forget that many people are beaten down by life. They
have very little that encourages them, and someone being kind
to them gives them hope. From that small act of service, we are
pointing them to Christ.

A number of books have been written about evangelicals
losing their influence in society. These books focus on the lack
of biblical thinking about what's going on in our society. But a
lack of biblical thinking is not the only problem. One of the
leaders of this movement is a seminary professor who refuses to
speak to the president of his institution because he disagrees with
some of the policies that the president and the board have decided
upon. Another man is the president of a Christian organization
that was censured and put on probation by an accrediting agency
for unethical behavior. Another man in this movement had to be
confronted by a pastor for mistreating people.

It is praiseworthy to talk about biblical thinking, biblical
thought processes, and a biblical worldview. But to concern

ourselves with these issues while we treat others disrespectfully destroys our credibility. While biblical thinking is important, so is biblical *living*. The crisis of Christians in our society
is not so much in the way we think about Christianity but in the
way we live it out.

Too often we forget that we are sinners saved by grace,
therefore we need to extend grace to other people. This doesn't
mean we don't have standards or we don't stand up for them.
Somehow we need to find a way to hold onto our Christian
convictions without letting go of Christlike character. When our
defense of truth lacks compassion, we end up pushing people
away. The problem is not the people who are being pushed
away but the people who are doing the pushing. The problem
is that we are asking for born-again behavior from people who
aren't, expecting a nation to follow Christ when it lacks the
power of Jesus Christ in the lives of its citizens.

Far too many followers of Jesus express their outrage at
what's going on in society by mounting moral crusades against
the heathen. Don't get me wrong; the convictions of Christ
demand that we stand up for truth. But the character of Christ
also requires us to weep over Jerusalem—or Washington—
not overwhelm those cities with vast armies of indignation. If
we're going to be people characterized by kindness, we need
to care to the point of brokenheartedness over what is going
on in our society. People who are most effective in relating their
faith are people who are as full of grace as they are of truth—
in short, people like Christ.

Unfortunately, people like Christ are a minority, not only in
society but in the church. Take this particular church as an
example. When one of my seminary professors moved to the
Chicago area to take a teaching position, he left his family in
another state until they sold their home. During the interim he
lived in the student dormitory. One Wednesday night he went
to a church Bible study, entering from the back of the auditorium shortly before the study began and sitting a few rows

from the back. Because he was a visitor, he didn't realize that there was another entrance near the front of the church that the study group usually used. Everyone else came in from the front of the building and sat near the front. "Some of the people looked back at me peculiarly," he recalled. The pastor came in from another door, led the Bible study, and when he finished, went back out through that door. The other people attending the study left through the front door, and the professor was left standing by himself. "I left that Bible study more lonely than when I came," he remarked, "because I had come to be with a group of people that I thought might reach out to encourage me, and no one said one word."

The word that God speaks is most often spoken through the lives of people—a word that has been made flesh by our actions, actions sometimes as slight as the shaking of a hand, a smile, a simple hello. As we think about reaching our communities for Christ, we must realize that one of the greatest ways we can touch people is through kindness.

KINDNESS COMES FROM THE HOLY SPIRIT

Where do we start in this ministry of kindness? We start with the truth. We start by realizing that much of our life is not an expression of kindness and by acknowledging that we need help. One of the beautiful things about the Bible is that it meets us where we are and offers us that help. It helps us understand our attitudes and how they fall short of the attitudes God wants us to have. Once we recognize that, it opens us up to a whole new way of God working in our lives.

Kindness is not a character quality buried deep in our lives that we have to excavate. It's not something we build one brick at a time. It's organic, something that grows within us. More accurately, it is *grown* within us by the work of the Holy Spirit.

When I saw the woman on the plane, whom I mentioned at the beginning of this chapter, treat the disfigured passenger so rudely, I was so offended that I wanted to pop her right in the chops. It would have felt so good, but it wouldn't have been kind. Not to her, not to the other passengers, and not to my family. My responsibility was to acknowledge my feelings and then pray, "Lord, I can't have the attitude toward this woman that I should have except through Your working in my life. Please work in me so I will have an attitude of kindness."

As the Spirit of God produces the fruit of kindness in our lives, we will begin to recognize that God is in the business of meeting needs and wants to meet those needs through our acts of kindness. If you like the game of basketball, you are familiar with National Basketball Association player Dennis Rodman. For those of you who don't know basketball, Dennis Rodman will come to one game with his hair colored green, the next game purple, the next game red, and the next game all those colors. He's notorious not only for his flamboyant hairstyles and clothing but also for his combative behavior. I think Dennis Rodman is a little weird, and I said as much to a friend of mine who is a former athlete.

His response nailed me to the wall: "I have great compassion for Dennis Rodman. In fact, I'm praying that God would bring someone into his life who could talk to him about Christ."

Do you see the difference in attitude? While I'm thinking Dennis Rodman is weird, my friend is praying for him. His *attitude* of kindness is producing an *act* of kindness, which in this case is prayer.

The most obvious example of God's kindness toward us was when He sent Jesus Christ to die on the cross for our sins. With that as our example, we need to ask ourselves, "Are we people of kindness, and how is that kindness shown to others?"

CHAPTER 7

REPENTANCE

WHILE OUR FAMILY WAS VACATIONING ON A LAKE IN northern Minnesota, our college-aged children reminisced about the pressures they felt during childhood because their father was a pastor. Michael told the story of how he and a young boy, whose family attended our church, got in trouble one day at elementary school.

What the two boys had done was not a major infraction. They hadn't plotted to lock the principal in his office and overthrow the school. It was simply a youngsters' prank, deserving a reprimand, nothing more. But when the teacher scolded them, she told Michael that because he was the son of a pastor, the school authorities expected more from him.

As a pastor's son, Michael felt he was the victim of a double standard. He felt he had been judged by a higher standard than the one by which other people judged themselves. It didn't seem fair. And it didn't seem to square with his understanding of Christ's teaching. Michael was right, for Jesus said: "Do not judge, or you too will be judged. For in the same way you judge others, you will be judged, and with the measure you use, it will be measured to you. Why do you look at the speck of sawdust in your brother's eye and pay no attention to the plank in your own eye? How can you say to your brother, 'Let me take the speck out of your eye,' when all the time there is a plank in your own eye? You hypocrite, first take the plank out of your own eye, and then you will see clearly to remove the speck from your brother's eye" (Matthew 7:1-5).

EXAMINE OUR OWN BEHAVIOR FIRST

We can't escape value judgments—nor should we—but those judgments should be based on a consistent standard. Jesus gave us not only a consistent but an exacting standard when He said that we are to examine ourselves first. It is much more tempting and much less troublesome to judge others. As natural as that is, though, it is wrong.

When Jesus said we are not to judge others, He was not saying that we are not to be aware of others' faults, and He was not saying that we are not to have standards by which we evaluate them. What He *was* saying was that we are not to judge others more harshly than we would judge ourselves, that we are not to judge without mercy, without love, or without prayer on behalf of the person in question.

When we see something wrong in another person's life, the first thing we are to do is to look at our own life. Maybe we think the President is a liar, maybe we don't like the Governor's stand on abortion, maybe we don't like how a minister carries out his responsibilities, maybe we think our adult children are not disciplining our grandchildren correctly. The list is endless. But before we take a hard look at the list, we need to take an honest look at ourselves. Is there any unconfessed sin in our life? Any attitudes that are wrong? Any behavior that needs to change?

Many of us would never steal a paper clip from our employer because the Bible says not to steal, but how many of us follow what the Bible says about examining our own lives before talking to other people about theirs? The reason we don't is that most of us don't like to look in the mirror. In his book *How to Win Over Worry*, John Haggai's thesis is that if we can keep our eyes focused on the other guy's problems and the things he is doing wrong, then we do not have to look at or deal with our own issues.[1] George Will, the political writer and commentator, said, "People only feel half alive when they aren't indignant; when they are indignant, then they feel alive."[2]

The glare of indignation, though, should be focused on our own heart, first and foremost. After that light has allowed us to see clearly enough to remove the log from our own eyes, then and only then does Jesus give us the freedom to remove the specks from the eyes of others.

LISTEN TO CRITICISM

It's hard for some people to examine themselves with the scrutiny that Jesus commands. For many years Dennis Eckersley, the famous baseball pitcher, was controlled by alcohol. His wife, Nancy, says of him during that time, "He was really bad. I asked myself all the time why I stayed with him. . . . I think it was because I could still see that he was a good, caring person. But that person was getting smaller and smaller."

Then something happened. "It was between Christmas and New Year's after the 1986 season," Eckersley recounted. "Nancy was off on a modeling assignment, and I was taking care of Mandee, who was 10 at the time. We were staying over at Nancy's sister's house in Connecticut. Well, one night I put on a real premeditated drunk. I was awful, and with Mandee there, too. What I didn't know was that D.J., Nancy's sister, was filming the whole thing.

"The next day I stumbled downstairs, and there's this video of me on TV. I'm watching myself in horror, saying to D.J., 'Please turn that off, please turn that off.' But she wouldn't, no matter how much I pleaded with her. So I had to watch this drunk who was me. And that was it. That was the wake-up call."[3]

Not all of us are fortunate enough to have a sister-in-law like Eckersley had who videotapes our worst moments so we can take a sobering look at ourselves. But maybe if somehow we could see our behavior the way others see it, it would be the wake-up call we need.

Major league baseball player Dwight Gooden finally got the wake-up call he needed after nine years of drug abuse. While discussing his need for treatment, he said, "I wanted to be open with people. You've got to be honest with yourself."[4]

Gooden is not as profound as Jesus, but he does put his finger on one vital truth: We need to quit playing games, quit ignoring the warnings we receive, quit blaming others, quit judging others—and take a good hard look at ourselves.

DON'T JUDGE

Aside from Jesus' warning not to judge, there are at least three other reasons why we should not rush to judgment.

Our perceptions may be wrong. No one is perfect, and we've all been in situations where we've misunderstood what someone said or did. If we draw conclusions based on a misunderstanding, we may incorrectly judge a person. We'd all be better off if we were a little more humble about our abilities to perceive situations correctly.

We may not have all the facts. I know of a situation where a man judged the actions of the board of a church hundreds of miles from where he lived. He did not have all the facts—indeed he had very few—but he thought he had the right to judge. He was very vocal about his views, but in the final analysis, he was completely wrong because he didn't have some crucial information. Proverbs 18:17 warns us that "the first to present his case seems right, till another comes forward and questions him." Such a rush to judgment can only succeed in pushing the truth headlong over a cliff.

Only God is totally impartial. It is impossible to be completely impartial, so we cannot judge with complete fairness. To some degree or another, we all show partiality. Often we are not as firm as we should be with those we like, while we are firmer than we should be with those we don't.

When the president of an institution was fired by his board, one of the key employees opposed the board's decision. Because the employee was partial to the president, he couldn't accept his friend's firing. When the successor was hired, the employee immediately had a bad attitude toward the new president. His inability to be impartial colored his relationship with the board, the new president, and the former president.

Although only God is totally impartial, that doesn't mean our tendency toward partiality—which is to say, our humanity—should keep us from entering the debate about values. *How* we enter the debate, though, is crucial, as Tony Winterowd noted in his doctoral dissertation at Talbot Seminary:

> All too often, we hear about Christians attacking
> another person's position with such a mean spirit
> that it violates Peter's exhortation to defend one's
> faith with "gentleness and respect." I have seen this
> firsthand with a friend of mine. The friend was a can-
> didate for the senior pastor position at a large church.
> The church offered him the position, but he turned it
> down because of a number of unhealthy issues the
> elder board and congregation had yet to deal with as
> a result of the previous pastor's departure. Not
> believing that anyone would turn the position down,
> members of the congregation began rumors concern-
> ing the soundness and orthodoxy of my friend's the-
> ology—rumors that were completely untrue.[5]

In a column in *Christianity Today,* Philip Yancey also addressed this issue of Christians attacking other believers:

> What has infected the Christian community with such outright meanness? The tactics used by some of the critics remind me of the worst attacks of Joseph McCarthy and the Reverend Carl McIntire, my heroes as I grew up in Southern fundamentalism. It was only later that I learned to recognize their conspiracy theories as a house of cards based on rumor, innuendo and guilt by association. I sense the same dynamic at work today [in the Christian community].[6]

When we rush to judgment, we disobey God and fail to further His kingdom. Jesus did not instruct us to deal with our own sins first simply so we can better see the speck in another person's eye and yank it out (Matthew 7:5). The sense of the Greek word in that passage, translated "take out" or "cast out," is a nonviolent type of extraction. We are to remove the speck, but we are to do it *gently*.

PROVIDE LOVING HELP

A man I knew went to his pastor to discuss an issue, and the pastor got defensive. But the man responded, "I love you, Pastor. That is why I came. People who do not love you would not come so openly." Unlike negative judging, the "speck removal" that Jesus speaks of is not destructive. Truth and restoration are key to what Jesus is describing. The issue is to remove the speck in someone else's eye in order to help the person.

This plays itself out in many ways. My friend, former colleague, and senior fellow at The Murdock Charitable Trust, Dr. Steve Nicholson, observes,

Christian people are the last people to think they are involved in politics or games. But they get caught up in it due to a sense of loyalty, prudence, protecting the faith, and alliances, and because they reach out to like-minded people. It is a sin endemic to social life and organizations because we hide from responsibilities and the realities of who we are and how we behave. . . . People are not crisp equations like engineering. If politics is the art of the possible, then nothing is unethical because the issue is to get it done, without any concern about how it gets done.

I was thinking about how much Jesus valued relationships. He said, "If your brother has aught against you, go to him and make it right."

How often in the flesh we would tell our friends or ourselves, "No, you are not going. You did not do anything wrong, and if he is mad, he can come and talk to you." That is what we would say, but that is not what Jesus said. We look at the responsibility. Jesus looks at the relationship. So if we are going to follow Jesus, then we must be willing to look beyond prevailing sentiment and wisdom and do what *He* says.

Some people recommend studying various personality styles to learn how to deal with and accept people who are different from us. Although I am a strong believer in this and have taught leadership styles in my doctoral courses, we must recognize that understanding personality styles also can degenerate into tolerating sin. People need to be told when they are wrong.

Consider the case of the university president who had a professor with a personality problem. This famous professor was an excellent teacher, but he was also an extraordinary troublemaker. The president was afraid to lose him. He thought enrollment would drop if the professor left, so in the name of working with the man's personality, he placated him by giving in to his demands. As a result, the professor didn't leave, at least not then. But he didn't mature, either. Parenthetically, when he did leave, enrollment increased anyway.

Why are we so quick to placate? Sometimes, as in the case with the professor, it's because we are afraid of the consequences to our organization. Other times, we simply don't care enough, either about the institution or about the individual, to confront. Admittedly, in the heat of battle and in the context of a pressure-filled business day, crisis management is necessary. When a building is engulfed in flames, for example, we need to evacuate, not confront the building superintendent about fire-code violations. But in the normal course of events, we need to manage people, too. And we need to manage them in a way that helps them mature, in the way that Proverbs advises: "Better is open rebuke than hidden love" (27:5).

Such a commitment isn't easy, though. And it's seldom convenient. It takes time because the other person may ask for an explanation. It takes energy because the other person may get angry. It takes courage because the other person may reject you. In spite of all it takes, it is still the best way to go. And in my opinion, the *only* way to go.

When Someone Refuses to See

I am always amazed at how hard people work to protect themselves from the truth about their behavior—a truth that everyone around them seems to see. Instead of making that admission, they charge ahead, oblivious to the effects of their behavior on the people around them.

For example, consider this man's experience: "I had a conflict with someone like that once. Unsure if everything had been resolved, I wrote the man, asking him if we were in fellowship. The apostle John wrote that if we walk in God's light, then 'we have fellowship with one another' (1 John 1:7), so this issue was very important to me. I didn't get a response, so I wrote again, and yet again. After writing four letters and still not receiving a response, I put the issue aside.

"Sixteen months later, I talked about this situation in a speech on reconciliation and said that sometimes when people will not discuss issues, we must assume that we have done all we can and move forward without looking back in guilt. A week later a man named Bob came to me and said that he had applied all the principles from the speech and reconciled with a man after years of a broken relationship.

"Driving home from that meeting, I told my wife that if God could work in Bob's situation, He could work in the broken relationship I had unsuccessfully tried to restore. That night I got on an airplane to fly two thousand miles. Only three of the seats on the plane were empty. When I located mine, it was next to the man who had refused to answer my letters. I could not believe it. He was right next to me. After some small talk, I plunged into a discussion of the situation. I asked if he had gotten my letters.

"'I have no desire to respond,' he said, almost exploding. 'I choose not to keep the correspondence going.'

"I knew enough not to react to his words, so I quietly said, 'In my last correspondence I asked if we are in fellowship.'

"He responded by saying that fellowship with me was not important to him. I thought, *There. It's out. He has exposed his spiritual immaturity. It is over. Unless God works in his life, nothing will change. I do not have to fix him.* And I went to work on a project I'd brought along.

"Later, a friend of his told a colleague of mine about the conversation, but the story my colleague heard was completely different from what had happened. Apparently the man I had tried to reconcile with said, 'We had a good talk. We agreed that we would never be friends, but we settled our differences.'"

I honestly do not know how to resolve this type of situation.

It is not just a matter of not seeing eye to eye with someone. It's a matter of someone not having eyes to see. Some people just can't look at themselves very honestly—a selective blindness of some sort. As a result, they always seem to be changing their stories to fit the facts, or the facts to fit their story.

A pastor I know was sitting in a meeting with some people from his congregation to discuss a project they thought would enrich the church's ministry. Later he was giving a ride home to a fairly new member of the congregation who was a recent convert to Christ. As they drove, the passenger said, "May I ask you a question? Why is Adam so angry? It seems that he sits passively with a huge pot of anger just below the surface and anytime anything is said that he does not like or agree with, his anger expresses itself in harsh language, stubbornness, intractability, and unkindness, to say nothing of his hostile body language. Why is that behavior tolerated in the church when it seems so wrong? Why is he allowed to be a leader in the church when he has that apparent anger problem?"

The pastor tried to give an answer, but, in truth, he didn't have one. Later, one of the other pastors on the staff had the opportunity to approach the man about his anger. After Adam spoke to him harshly, the pastor quietly asked, "Adam, are you angry?"

"No, I am not," he snapped.

Later, when Adam's wife asked him to tell his adult daughter what the pastor had asked him, Adam responded in an equally harsh tone, "That exchange will *never* be discussed again."

All too frequently, the church is the scene of such exchanges. I know that the guy who writes the book is supposed to have all the answers. The truth is, I don't. I don't know what you do with people who refuse to admit they're wrong. The best advice I can give doesn't come from my wisdom but from Solomon's. In Proverbs, he repeatedly tells us not to waste our time with a fool (26:4), that a fool will not listen (23:9), that a fool will not change (17:10), and that a fool will not grow (18:2). If a person refuses to come to grips with an obvious weakness, sometimes it is best just to walk away.

Strong-willed people don't like to be told they're wrong, and if told, they usually don't admit it. This kind of confrontation is not so much about the truth as it is about the psychological makeup of the person who has been challenged.

Jack Nicklaus, the king of golf, is not only regarded as the greatest golfer to have played the game but also as one of the most strong-willed. One of his fiercest competitors has been Hale Irwin. Irwin says this about Nicklaus:

> Jack's greatest ability, other than his playing skills, is that he's very sure of himself. Even when he can be proved wrong, Jack in his mind is right. You don't have a discussion or an argument with Jack. You might talk to Jack, but ultimately he believes what he believes. The people around Jack pretty much recognize him as being a forceful individual. And some people who may be a bit wishy-washy in their opinions will not stand up to Jack. I think he recognizes in me that I'm not a wishy-washy guy. I, too, am relatively strong-minded. So, we have had a great relationship.[7]

The point of my quoting Irwin is not to demean Nicklaus, because I've never met him. I certainly wish I could golf like he does. But isn't it true that we all know far too many people who say they are followers of Christ who have to be hit over the head with a nine iron before they will admit the truth? In the case of these people the issue is not about truth—it is about winning and not having to say they were wrong. I think we should all be asking God to develop enough humility in us that we are willing to listen to what people say whether or not they are as strong-willed as Hale Irwin. Responding to and growing in the truth should be the issue—not winning.

With those people for whom winning *is* the issue, and the only issue, truth does not win out. *They* do. And when they do, the only alternative left to us is to walk away. The idea of walking away from such people is reinforced by a discussion Jesus had with His disciples about the Pharisees. The Pharisees may be the most blatant example we have of religious people who stubbornly refused to see the error of their ways. The disciples came to Jesus, asking if He realized that something He said had offended the Pharisees. Jesus answered, "Every plant that my heavenly Father has not planted will be pulled up by the roots. Leave them; they are blind guides. If a blind man leads a blind man, both will fall into a pit" (Matthew 15:13-14). When we have made every effort to restore a relationship and it doesn't work out, perhaps it is time to leave the matter in God's hands and simply move on.

Bill Curry, a fine Christian man who once coached football at the University of Kentucky, was faced with such a decision. One summer one of his players was shot as he sat on his porch. The gun was a hunting rifle. The shot was a single bullet to the head. The player died instantly. The crime remains unsolved, with no clues and no suspects.

During the season, an anonymous call to the athletic department threatened the lives of Curry's wife and children. The FBI insisted the family leave town for their own protection. Curry said the death threat caused a feeling in him that he did not know existed. He learned to understand that there are people in the world like that and they needed to be forgiven so he could focus on the good people in life.

The coach had a choice to make. He could spend the rest of his life trying to hunt down the criminals who had killed his player and threatened his family, or he could leave the criminals in God's hands and move on with his life. By choosing to move on, his life has been blessed with a freedom he never would have had if he had tried to take matters into his own hands.

There are some people and some situations we are actually called to walk away from. Paul mentions one such case in Titus 3:10: "Warn a divisive person once, and then warn him a second time. After that, have nothing to do with him." Though the advice is right, it doesn't mean we are to walk away from everyone who has differing opinions, even if the opinions are theological.

Obviously, we all have areas of weakness that we don't recognize. And while the Bible is our authority, gray areas exist where for centuries Christians have disagreed. We do not want to cut ourselves off from everyone who looks at the world in a slightly different way than we do. Discussing different views is both challenging and enlightening. And as long as the goal of enlightenment remains, and as long as the spirit of honesty remains, *we* should remain.

I was impressed by the spirit of honesty in an article I read on Dwight Gooden, who, after ruining his baseball career with drugs, tried to make a comeback. He asked a man to sponsor him in Alcoholics Anonymous. The man responded, "Are you serious about turning your life around? If you are not ready to recover, I am not interested. Talk is cheap. Stay clean for twenty-four hours, and I'll be impressed. Show me how desperately you want it."[8]

If the church of Jesus Christ is going to help its members grow, we must all be willing to be as honest with each other as that AA sponsor was with Gooden. Sheila Walsh wrote the book on honesty. Sheila gained fame working as Pat Robertson's co-host on the television program *The 700 Club*. On camera, she came across as a person with many answers for whom life in Christ was a total success. Off camera, though, she was dying. In her book, *Honestly*, she wrote,

> One of the questions I continue to wrestle with is "What is real faith?" I believe it will always be God's will to restore families, to mend broken lives so that we can continue to walk together. I hold that truth

close to my heart as I walk in a broken, fallen world. What I think we as the church lack, though, is a place to talk about how things really are. In our desire to be an inspiration to one another we often veil what is true, because what is true is not always inspirational. But hurting believers whose lives are in tatters often need real help. If we were able to put aside our need for approval long enough to be authentic, then, surely, we would be living as the church.[9]

PART TWO

HOW WE

NURTURE

UNCOMMON

GRACES

CHAPTER 8

BUILDING COMMUNITY

AMERICAN EVANGELICAL CHRISTIANITY SUFFERS FROM AN overemphasis on the individual. We stress personal salvation while forgetting that the biblical view of redemption includes both individuals and groups. We teach that spiritual growth emerges primarily from personal study and prayer, but we forget that a mature faith includes accountability, which requires other people. We go on solitary retreats to determine God's direction for our lives, only to be frustrated until we ask for help from a few close friends.

The Bible certainly encourages us to establish and maintain a personal relationship with God. However, both the Old and New Testaments also teach that the spiritual health of God's people should be evaluated by the condition of their social, political, economic, and religious institutions.

Discovering just how much emphasis God places on the group can be a shocking experience—so shocking to one man I know that he stopped reading the Old Testament for about two years, shortly after he became a Christian. He did this because he was horrified and confused by an incident recorded in Joshua 7.

"I barely knew who Jesus was and what He had done or taught," he explains. "I figured I would develop a more accurate picture of God by studying the life of Christ and the teachings of early Christian leaders than by trying to understand all the bizarre complexities of the Old Testament. I was afraid my whole view of God as a loving father who accepted me might get twisted before I understood what following Jesus was about. The God I saw at work in the story of Achan was not someone I could respect or trust."

Achan was a member of the tribe of Judah. He stole some of Jericho's plunder that was intended for the Lord's treasury. His disobedience resulted in Israel's defeat at the first battle of Ai. When discovered, he was taken out and stoned to death, along with his entire family and all their livestock.

I can sympathize with the man's feelings about that passage. It *is* confusing, even for many of us who have been in Christian professional work for years. What *is* clear about the passage is that it shows how God was concerned about the spiritual health of the group as well as that of the individual. Neither is this simply an Old Testament idea.

Shortly before the crucifixion, Jesus made this statement to His disciples: "A new command I give you: Love one another. As I have loved you, so you must love one another. By this all men will know that you are my disciples, if you love one another" (John 13:34-35). The identifying mark of Christians is not primarily their relationship with Jesus Christ but their relationships with each other. The spiritual health of the group continues to be an extremely important concept.

At the end of the apostle John's life, he was granted a glimpse of the future and was asked to pass on a series of warnings to the believers of his day. Located in the second and third chapters of Revelation, these warnings are given to congregations, not to individuals. The uncommon graces we have discussed in this book *do* affect our individual lives. But they are meant to go beyond that to affect the lives of those around us. Let's examine some specific strategies we can use to help unleash the power of grace that changes lives.

CARRY ONE ANOTHER'S BURDENS

A few years ago when I was working on a project for The Murdock Charitable Trust, we designed a study to determine the needs and attitudes of people in evangelical churches. We began with a list of five thousand people that we gave to a professional survey company. They used a random number generator to telephone 500 of those people, and they actually talked with 420 of them. One of the questions we asked was, "What is the number-one quality you're looking for in your pastor?" We assumed the answer would point toward something like biblical knowledge, preaching skills, or general leadership ability. We were astounded to learn that the number-one response was compassion.

For most of us, the simple demands of daily life overwhelm us in ways we couldn't have imagined fifty years ago. There are few places where we can go to escape from the storms of life. The thing most of us long for, above all else, is a safe haven where someone will really listen to us and treat us with compassion.

In today's society, the most important way we can affect those around us is to give them a safe place where they will be treated with compassion. Paul had that in mind when he wrote these words: "Brothers, if someone is caught in a sin, you who are spiritual should restore him gently. But watch yourself, or you also may be tempted. Carry each other's burdens, and in this way you will fulfill the law of Christ" (Galatians 6:1-2).

The word "burden" in verse 2 means a weight that is larger than normal. That's precisely what we are left with after the storms of life have rolled over us. Our most immediate need is for someone to help us carry those burdens. Life in a fallen world is never going to be problem-free or stress-free. Burdens are a normal part of life, even for those who have surrendered their lives to Christ. Paul himself knew what it meant to carry burdens. In 2 Corinthians he wrote, "For when we came into Macedonia, this body of ours had no rest, but we were harassed at every turn—conflicts on the outside, fears within" (2 Corinthians 7:5). That wasn't the end of the story, though. He went on to say, "But God, who comforts the downcast, comforted us by the coming of Titus" (verse 6). God sent another Christian to comfort Paul and his companions, to help them bear the physical and emotional burdens they were carrying.

The key to bearing burdens appears in Galatians 6:1 in the phrase, "restore him gently." The word "restore" is the same word that was used in that day to describe the action of a fisherman who was sitting on the shore mending his nets. These nets were too valuable to discard, and they got many holes in them from being pulled through the water full of fish, dragged into boats, and pulled across rocky beaches. Fishermen repaired their nets both because they were expensive to replace and so they would be strong enough to hold their catch. Paul says we should do the same for people around us, looking for ways to restore them to full capacity, because they are too valuable to discard.

For too many of us, life's burdens start tearing away at our nets at an early age. Twelve-year-old Samuel Graham was afraid to go to school. He felt this way despite the fact that he was an outstanding student. The problem was that his "friends" constantly teased him about his weight. At 174 pounds, Samuel was burdened by the condition of a 5'4" body, a burden he could no longer bear by himself. Samuel frequently attended church and played the piano during the service. One night after playing at church, he took part in an evening Bible study with his father and two younger brothers, Joshua and David. Afterward he went to bed.

Early the next morning, when most of his classmates were still sleeping, Samuel found a rope, a flashlight, and a step stool. He carried them out into the cold, dark back yard of his family's home, threw the rope over the limb of a tree, and hanged himself. His brothers found him later in the morning as they were getting ready for the first day of school. His father tried to revive him, but it was too late.[1]

Samuel Graham died because he was isolated from everyone around him by the shame and horror of his overweight body. He died because he did not know how to let someone help him bear his burden. Some of the burdens carried by those around us are carefully hidden. We will never have an opportunity to help carry them unless we demonstrate to others that we can be trusted with the knowledge of those burdens.

A safe place for us to lay down those burdens would be a place where we will be treated with compassion. Someplace like Mary Pipher's office. Some years ago, Dr. Pipher — a psychologist from Lincoln, Nebraska, who wrote the book *Reviving Ophelia*[2] — noticed a change in her counseling practice. Increasing numbers of her patients were middle-class, teenage girls who were struggling with self-mutilation. This disturbing practice is related to deep-seated self-hatred and is very difficult to treat. Dr. Pipher could have ignored this trend and focused on less complex problems. Instead, she chose to study the problem and make it a special emphasis in her practice. This cost a great deal of time, effort, and personal pain, but it made her uniquely qualified to bring healing to the lives of these tortured young women.

We must allow God to rearrange the furniture of our life so room can be made to help others. I was reminded of this recently when Susan and I spent some time in Sacramento visiting her oldest sister and her family. On our last day with them, just as Sharron and her husband, Jim Coulter, were getting ready to take us to the airport, a friend of theirs stopped by. It was obvious he wanted to discuss something privately, so the three excused themselves and moved to a room at the other end of the house. After about fifteen or twenty minutes, I began getting worried. I had no idea who the man was or what he wanted to talk about, but I did know that we needed to get to the airport.

Just then Sharron came into the room, crying. "Our friend just told us that his wife has cancer of the liver and it has spread to some of her other organs as well. It's terminal. I'm going to take you to the airport while Jim stays here with him."

It was a quiet and somber ride. About halfway to our destination, Sharron started talking about her friend's illness. "I've known her a long time, and I'm just beginning to realize that my life is about to change, along with hers. I'll be helping her with a lot of the things she's going to be facing over the next few months."

I was struck by the way she said this. There was no sense of self-pity or irritation at her friend for the pain and disorder she was bringing into Sharron's life. She was already counting the cost, already figuring out how to rearrange her life and adjust her other priorities to make room for her friend's needs. It is in moments like this that we discover the real strength or weakness of our spiritual lives. If we want the uncommon graces of God to flow through us, not only must we be willing to bear one another's burdens, but we must be willing to pay the price of bearing those burdens.

TREAT ONE ANOTHER IMPARTIALLY

In chapters 4 and 5 of his first letter to Timothy, Paul instructed his young friend on how to manage the practical business of a church congregation. In 5:21 he wrote, "I charge you, in the sight of God and Christ Jesus and the elect angels, to keep these instructions without partiality, and to do nothing out of favoritism."

The Greek word translated *partiality* means "inclined toward." It's a wonderful picture of how we usually treat each other. I'm inclined toward my wife, Susan. I'm inclined toward my daughter, Stephanie. I'm inclined toward my son, Michael. I favor them, take their side in a dispute, make them a high priority in my life—just as Al McGuire supposedly did with his family.

When Al McGuire was head basketball coach at Marquette University, his son Allie played for him the year the team won the national championship. Legend has it that the coach used to tell recruits who played Allie's position that they were going to have to be *much* better than his son if they were going to beat him out, because he was partial to his son.

Obviously it is honorable for me to be inclined toward my family, and it is honorable for the coach to be honest with recruits about how he would favor his son. We would even agree that this is an expression of love—and I suppose it is. But because we are human and imperfect, we are going to love imperfectly, and we are going to be partial, which means we will bend the standards to the advantage of the ones we love. But God is perfect, and this means He does not bend His standards to the advantage of anyone. This is why He is God. His standards are a constant, requiring all to grow. Our standards are somewhat flexible and may or may not require another person to grow.

Thus, we understand that impartiality starts with God and not with us. Paul wrote this in Romans: "For God does not show favoritism. All who sin apart from the law will also perish apart from the law, and all who sin under the law will be judged by the law" (2:11-12). A little later in the same letter, he also said, "God demonstrates his own love for us in this: While we were still sinners, Christ died for us" (5:8). In both His response to sin and His offer of redemption, God is totally impartial.

The experience of Peter in the early days of the church also bears this out. After God had challenged Peter's ideas of ritual cleanliness and sent him to the house of Cornelius, the Roman centurion, Peter had this to say: "I now realize how true it is that God does not show favoritism but accepts men from every nation who fear him and do what is right" (Acts 10:34-35).

This is a tough standard for us to live up to. Our world, both inside and outside the church, is permeated with favoritism.

There is racial prejudice, ethnic hatred, and a deep suspicion of those who are different from us. And there is always the assumption that God agrees with our biases. But what Martin Luther reportedly said dispels that assumption: "Your thoughts of God are too human. This is where most of us go astray. Our thoughts of God are not great enough. We fail to reckon with the reality of His limitless wisdom and power. Because we our-selves are limited and weak, we imagine that at some point God is, too, and we find it hard to believe that He is not. We think of God as too much like what we are."

It is easy for us to begin with our own standards and impose them on God, rather than accepting His standards and allowing ourselves to be changed into the image of His Son. Our view of God is incomplete. Most of us try to make God too white, too male, too American, and too rich.

But when the Holy Spirit grabs us, shakes us, and gets us to repent of our partiality, amazing things happen—like what happened some time ago in Eugene, Oregon. I was there for my thirty-year college reunion. I got into a conversation with a fraternity brother. Bill was not a person who had seemed interested in spiritual issues during college. As his story unfolded, it became clear that this had changed.

"When I was in high school," he began, "I got involved in Fellowship of Christian Athletes. Then when I got to college, I sort of moved away from that. After college I came down to the Bay area and started coaching football. Then my wife and I separated."

He continued, "On New Year's Eve some guys invited me to play basketball with them. What I didn't know was that we were going to be playing basketball at a church. What I also didn't know was that these men knew I was separated. They knew I was lonely and that my life was a mess. They didn't hold that against me. They just wanted me to enjoy their com-pany for an evening."

The men playing basketball with Bill that night were not

the only impartial group of Christians at work in that city. A little later in the discussion, Bill's wife Kathy joined us and began to tell her side of the story. While this group of men was reaching out to Bill, a group of women was reaching out to her. Eventually these two groups got Bill and Kathy back together. Then they got them some help for their marital problems. Next they encouraged them to get involved in a Bible study for couples.

But that's not the end of their story.

"Later we lost a child when he was just a year old," Bill said, glancing at Kathy.

She looked at me, and I could see the sadness of that loss brimming in her eyes. She said, "If we had not had our faith in Christ and if our friends had not reached out to us, we would never have gotten through the pain of that tragedy."

It's easy to avoid people who have turmoil in their lives. We don't feel safe around them. Maybe we're afraid their troubles will rub off on us, like some invisible plague. We fear for our own marriages, our own children, our own lives. We pull away from suffering and lean instead toward peace, comfort, success. Bill and Kathy are living vibrant Christian lives today, but only because some believing friends were willing to treat them with impartiality.

SPUR ONE ANOTHER ON

Another strategy we can use to unleash the power of uncommon graces into the lives of people around us is suggested by the author of the book of Hebrews:

> Therefore, brothers, since we have confidence to enter
> the Most Holy Place by the blood of Jesus, by a new
> and living way opened for us through the curtain,
> that is, his body, and since we have a great priest over

the house of God, let us draw near to God with a sincere heart in full assurance of faith, having our hearts sprinkled to cleanse us from a guilty conscience and having our bodies washed with pure water. Let us hold unswervingly to the hope we profess, for he who promised is faithful. And let us consider how we may spur one another on toward love and good deeds. (10:19-24)

Hebrews addresses one of the most difficult conflicts in the first-century church. Some Jewish Christians thought faith in Jesus Christ should be grafted onto the existing system of Jewish beliefs and practices. They believed this would fulfill Old Testament prophecy and deliver their nation from the hands of corrupt religious leaders. Other Jewish Christians and nearly all Gentile believers saw commitment to Christ as the first step into an entirely new system of belief based on God's grace and made real by the presence of the Holy Spirit. They saw this as a fulfillment of Old Testament prophecy. But they also saw the existing Jewish system as completely apostate and the Jewish nation as no longer relevant to God's plan for redeeming the world.

The former group of Jewish Christians constantly demanded that the Gentiles observe all sorts of dietary laws and other regulations set forth in the Old Testament, including the painful rite of circumcision. They often maintained a superior attitude toward their Gentile brothers and sisters, saying that only Jews could be true members of God's chosen people.

The Gentile believers weren't much better. They pointed to the freedom that grew out of the sacrifice of Jesus on the cross and maintained that there were no longer any rules of any kind they needed to follow. They looked for opportunities to offend the religious sensibilities of Jewish Christians. A few of them even started vicious rumors about all Jews being "Christ killers" and therefore unfit for membership in the new Christian community.

This was a volatile situation, as bad as anything any of us have ever seen in the American church of this century. The author of Hebrews addresses this problem in three ways. He spends the first ten chapters developing the argument that Jesus has brought an entirely new kind of redemption into the world as a fulfillment of all the best that God had revealed to the Jews in the Old Testament. Next he argues that all God's people throughout history are united in faith by Christ. Finally, he calls on them to support each other and be united in the suffering they are facing as Christ's followers.

The author's goal is to get Jewish and Gentile Christians to begin acting like a family. He wants them to find common ground so everyone can begin to grow together into the image of Jesus Christ. He wants them to "spur one another on to love and good deeds" (Hebrews 10:24).

Fast-forward two thousand years, and here is what that spurring on looks like in our culture. A few years ago I was officiating at the wedding of an old college friend. It was somewhat like a college reunion because of all the former students who showed up. I was having a good time, and I wasn't being too careful about some of the jokes I was making. At the rehearsal on Friday night, I managed to offend one of the women in the bridal party. I only learned about this because a friend came up and asked me, "Do you understand that you offended that woman?"

My mouth dropped open, and I stammered, "I didn't know that at all."

I went right over to the woman and said, "I'm terribly sorry. I did not mean to hurt you. I did not mean to offend you, and I am here to apologize and to ask you to forgive me." Then I held my breath, wondering how she was going to respond.

She put her arms around me, gave me a big hug, and said, "It's not a problem. I forgive you."

I would never have known there *was* a problem if my friend had not been courageous enough to "spur me on to love and good deeds." Unfortunately, not all the problems that develop within the church are as easy to remedy as the mistake I made at that wedding rehearsal. Some are more public and require a more public response, as the following story illustrates.

I have a friend named Alan who spent the first twenty years of his spiritual journey in the same church. Alan came to faith at sixteen and by his late twenties was considered a leader in the congregation. He was involved in the music ministry, taught Sunday school, led small groups, and even was involved in a national singles ministry. Then one night, at a church business meeting, he made a terrible mistake.

"It was one of several meetings we had held about changing the church constitution," Alan said. "The whole process was very controversial, and people were getting very upset. I had always considered myself a voice for moderation, but that night something snapped in me."

Alan had spent most of the evening listening to the ebb and flow of the debate, but he stopped listening when an older woman got up and made some disparaging remarks about a friend of his who was a strong supporter of the new constitution.

"I just totally lost it," he said. "I got up and verbally blew her out the back door. I did everything except call her the spawn of the Devil. What's most frightening to me in retrospect is that I had no idea what I had just done. Some people even congratulated me on the speech."

Fortunately, one person didn't. Alan's friend, Dave, called him a few days later and asked if they could meet. Dave had watched Alan grow up in that church, had been thankful for his influence on two of his sons, and had spent three years in a small growth group that Alan had a part in leading. So there was a strong bond between them.

"What I remember most about that meeting with Dave was how calm he was. He never raised his voice, never berated me. He just said, 'I was very disappointed in you last Sunday night.'

His words stunned me and shamed me, but in a good way. When he explained what I had done to that woman, I just sat there and cried."

Alan asked Dave what he needed to do to make the situation right. Dave suggested that the most appropriate thing would be to get up at the next meeting and ask the woman's forgiveness as well as the congregation's. That's exactly what happened.

"It was strange, really. I told the pastor I had something I needed to make right with the congregation. I didn't feel any fear as I was walking to the front or as I was speaking. It felt like I had done it before somehow. Like it was foreordained."

What struck me about Alan's story was that after he finished, many people from both sides of the constitution debate came up to him and thanked him for what he had said and done. An act of religious terrorism became an opportunity for surrender. And the act of surrender became an occasion for healing, all because a friend had spurred Alan on to love and good deeds.

SUBMIT TO ONE ANOTHER

It has always struck me as odd, even tragic, that the passage in Ephesians 5:21-33, which teaches about submission, has been used by flagrant abusers of power to justify their actions. It has been the primary proof-text for many corrupt exercises of hierarchical privilege in the two-thousand-year history of the church. The passage has been used to justify the mistreatment of wives by their husbands, the abuse of children by their parents, and the killing of employees by their employers. It has even been used to justify the institution of slavery.

Paul's intent was something else entirely. Contained in this passage is a radical model for mutual respect and service that grows directly from the intervention of the Holy Spirit in our lives. "Be filled with the Spirit," Paul wrote. Then he described what that would look like, finishing with these words: "Submit to one another out of reverence for Christ" (Ephesians 5:18-21). The Christian community is to be characterized at all its levels and in all its relationships by the discipline of mutual submission.

What is submission? The Greek word is a military term. It means "to rank under." In the kingdom of God, people aren't divided into first- and second-class citizens. We are to rank all other people as more important than ourselves.

In a society that has an anti-authoritarian mentality, it's not easy being submissive. And living in a society where so many of our elected leaders live lives that are inconsistent with their oaths of office also makes submission difficult. But even though submission is not easy, the Bible tells us it is an identifying mark of someone who is filled with the Spirit.

Jesus gave us a striking example of this in John 13. He washed the feet of all the disciples, including Judas'. It's hard for us to imagine ourselves in that situation, but would you kneel down and wash the feet of a person you knew was going to betray you? I'm not sure I would. Yet Jesus did. The proof that our lives are lived in reverence to Christ is that we submit them to each other.

Submitting ourselves to each other. I grew up in a Christian family, but from the time I was a little kid, one of my uncles called people in government work "stupid." They never knew how to do the job, he would complain, and they never built the highways right, among other things.

If you hear any message often enough as a child, you begin to develop similar attitudes. In college, though, I came to faith in Christ and face to face with Paul's teachings about submission. I realized that the attitude of arrogance and disrespect, which had been nurtured in me by part of my family, was in direct conflict with the Word of God. It had to go. When Paul wrote that we must submit to each other, I think he meant that some things in our lives must go and other things must take their place. He meant we're to be careful how we speak to each other. He meant we're to be considerate toward one another. And he meant we're to compliment each other.

This is not the message we get from society. That message tells me that if I don't like you, I can say anything about you I want. If I don't agree with you, ethically *or* economically, I can treat you like a stooge. Unfortunately, we find that same spirit in the church. When we disagree with other believers, we often treat them rudely and disrespectfully. When that happens, fissures in the church can become splits.

Instead, when we disagree with each other, we must ask ourselves, *Am I going to the person with whom I disagree in an attitude that reflects the beauty and purity of Jesus Christ?* When we submit to each other, we won't always agree, but we should always treat one another with respect and consideration.

A man I know has a daughter who is a recovering heroin addict. The man and his wife go to NarAnon meetings to learn more about the struggles of having a family member who is an addict. He says that one entire meeting was devoted to sixteen very loving parents who talked about the guilt they felt because, in many cases, they didn't trust their adult addicted children. The addicts have lied to, stolen from, and abused their parents in order to get more money for drugs. My friend said that there was absolutely no criticism of parents who felt the tremendous inner tension of loving their kids but not trusting them.

He continued his story with these words:

> Driving home from that meeting, I felt so good. The group affirmed everyone in his or her struggle to do right. There was no criticism of anyone who disagreed. On the other hand, I thought about what I often see in the church and in Christian circles, and that made me sad. Sad that people not in attendance are criticized. Sad that people who show up and disagree are demeaned. Sad that people—Christian

people—attack each other instead of help each other. Maybe in the NarAnon group there is a genuine humility and a very real need for God, where in the church there is a lack of humility and little need to depend on God.

Submitting ourselves to authorities. The idea of submitting to each other includes submitting to those who have spiritual authority over us. Both the writers of Hebrews and Peter make this quite clear (Hebrews 13:17, 1 Peter 5:5). The idea of submitting to spiritual authorities is not very popular in the church today. The anti-authoritarian attitude we have in our society follows us right into church, and we act as though no one has authority over us. Some members throw tantrums like a defiant child: "I don't care what the church says, I don't care what the elders say, I don't care what the staff says—I'm going to do what *I* want to do."

A few years ago, the elders in a large church made a decision. Twelve members of the church did not agree with the decision, so they wrote a letter stating that the elders' decision was not of God. And they mailed it to everyone on the membership list.

I have no problem with a person saying, "The elders made the wrong decision." I have no problem with a person saying, "I think the decision the elders made was outside the will of God." But these people never asked the elders if they would discuss the decision with them. Instead they went right to the congregation. They showed no respect for the authority of the elders over their church. In essence, they were saying that they don't even submit to God, because they didn't follow the chain of command He put over them.

How to develop submissiveness. If our Christian community is to be a place where we are submitting to each other, we need to grow in our sensitivity to the Holy Spirit. We need His help.

First, we need to keep a check on our attitude toward other people. We do that by stepping back and asking ourselves some honest questions. Are we committed to disagree with each other in dignity? Are we committed to speak the truth about—and *to*—each other in love?

Second, we need to remember that we speak with more that just our mouths. When our daughter, Stephanie, was two years old, a missionary friend visited us. His name is Lee Carlson, and he stretches about 6'4". When Stephanie came into the room, she ran up to the chair where he was sitting and grabbed the knees of his pants, singing out, "Lee, Lee, Lee!" Instantly, he got down on his knees so he could look Stephanie in the eye.

That small incident moved me. A tall, intelligent man honored a little girl by getting down to her level. Without saying a word, he communicated that what she had to say was important. Too often, the nonverbal messages we send say just the opposite.

Third, we need to make sure that our speech is full of the love and grace of Christ. In his essay *The Weight of Glory*, C. S. Lewis had this to say about the way we should speak to one another:

> It is a serious thing to live in a society of possible gods and goddesses, to remember that the dullest and most uninteresting person you talk to may one day be a creature which, if you saw it now, you would be strongly tempted to worship, or else a horror and a corruption such as you now meet, if at all, only in a nightmare. All day long we are, in some degree, helping each other to one or other of these destinations. It is in the light of these overwhelming possibilities, it is with the awe and the circumspection proper to them, that we should conduct all our dealings with one another, all friendships, all loves,

all play, all politics. There are no ordinary people. You have never talked to a mere mortal. Nations, cultures, arts, civilization—these are mortal, and their life is to ours as the life of a gnat. But it is immortals whom we joke with, work with, marry, snub and exploit— immortal horrors or everlasting splendours.[3]

The work of building community takes a lifetime. But the worth of the community is taken into eternity. It's some of the hardest work we will ever do. It's also some of the most worthwhile.

CHAPTER 9

ESTABLISHING CIRCUIT BREAKERS

IT WAS SUPPOSED TO BE A MEETING FOR BELIEVERS. THE SPEAKER was invited to tell about his ministry and how God was using it in other people's lives. He is a fairly gracious and non-critical person; however, he later told me that he wished he had never gone. By the time he left, he felt dirty and defiled. Why?

The meeting began well enough. A person prayed for God's blessing and reaffirmed the group's desire to be Christlike. But then the government, elected officials, laws and policies, and other people who disagreed with the group's prevailing sense of right and wrong were discussed in critical and demeaning ways. The speaker said the level of self-righteousness was suffocating. It reminded him of nature shows on television where gorillas stand around beating on their chests, ignoring their own bad breath. His final comment was, "I do not care to associate with those people, whether or not they *are* Christians."

Why is it that so many people who claim to be followers of Jesus Christ live lives that are so offensive? Why is it that so many people who claim to be Christians are themselves so unChristlike? Many of these people are not looking at themselves. They are not honestly appraising the effect they have on other people's lives. It is as though they are unable to see themselves as others see them. M. Scott Peck would say they are not assuming personal responsibility and instead are choosing to blame others.[1]

This refusal to accept responsibility gets to the heart of the issue of circuit breakers. Just as circuit breakers in our homes break the flow of electricity when there is a power surge or another electrical problem, personal circuit breakers are those people whom God uses to break the flow of destructive behavior in our lives.

Each of us *needs* circuit breakers in our lives.

And God has called us to *be* circuit breakers in the lives of others.

Why We Need Circuit Breakers

We all have times when too much of ourselves and not enough of Christ shows through. We need people who love us enough to point out our shortcomings, inconsistencies, and sins so that the image of Christ isn't obscured.

We need circuit breakers to help us look at ourselves. It is impossible for us to grow if we don't recognize the areas where we need to change. But seeing ourselves with complete honesty is impossible without input from those around us. "The heart is deceitful above all things and beyond cure. Who can understand it?" observed God through the prophet Jeremiah (17:9).

In an ideal world, all of us could see the areas in our lives we need to change. In the real world, though, we build walls around those areas. Why? A number of reasons. Because we are fearful. Because we are protecting ourselves. Because we have been hurt in the past and are determined not to be hurt again.

Jesus described the person who was able to be completely honest with God, with himself, and with others as pure in heart (Matthew 5:8). A totally impure person is dishonest with God, with himself, and with others. Most of us live somewhere between these two extremes. In one area or another, we are all self-deceived. We will say, *I did okay. . . . It is what I felt. . . . My doctrine was correct*, but we never really answer the question, *Was I behaving in a Christlike way?*

One of my best friends in college told me that he needed to consider leaving his extremely stressful job. He reached this conclusion one night when he went to tell his daughter good-night. As he sat beside her bed, he said, "I'm sorry I yelled at you. I've had a bad day at work." She looked up at him and said, "Dad, you have a lot of bad days at work."

His daughter acted as a circuit breaker. With that one sentence, she gave him the opportunity to set aside his excuses and take an honest look at how the stress of his job was affecting him.

We need circuit breakers to help us see how our weaknesses cause us to behave. It is one thing to look at ourselves in general terms and see that we are, say, impatient. It is another thing to catch ourselves snapping at our children, saying very specific and hurtful words and creating very specific reactions. We all develop bad habits—things we say and do that are contrary to the way Christ lived. Because these behaviors are habitual, we may not notice them any more than we notice our tendency to tap our fingers or chew on a pencil. The cause of these behaviors is often rooted deep in our personality, and to unearth it we sometimes need the help of professionals. There are a number of wonderful tools that professionals use to help people understand their specific type of personality. Dr. David Merrill suggests there are four primary types: *Drivers, Analyticals, Expressives,* and *Amiables.*[2]

My personality style tends toward being a *Driver.* When I am attacked, I tend to hit back. That predisposes me toward conflict. *Amiables* are just the opposite. When they face pressured situations, they tend to pull away. But that tendency leaves issues unresolved. *Expressives* can be so expansive with their speech that people wonder if they're even telling the truth. *Analyticals* control others by asking an inordinate number of questions and not dealing with the issues.

No one style is right. Let me illustrate what I mean by drawing an analogy with music. Some people like classical, some like country western, some like rock and roll, some like jazz. There isn't a good or bad style of music. It is a matter of taste. But if you play any one of those types of music full blast, the effect will be distracting at best and deafening at worst. It's the same with personality styles.

Knowing my personality style as a *Driver* lets me pray and prepare to react in the most positive manner possible. But I still need the help of circuit breakers to point out when my predisposition toward hitting back has become a metaphorical punch. Because of how I'm wired, I start swinging before I realize it. My wife, Susan, has been particularly helpful to me in this area. One way in which she helps me keep my *Driver* tendencies from crossing the line is by asking, "Is what you are doing consistent with what you said on Sunday in your sermon?"

Sometimes it takes a question like that to throw the switch on behavior that's overloading the circuits. That's why circuit breakers are so important, for as David said in Psalm 19:12, "We all have blind spots; we don't know ourselves as well as others know and see us" (paraphrase mine).

We need circuit breakers to help us take responsibility for ourselves. We've all experienced situations in which we become so angry or frustrated or upset that we react inappropriately. Or a change in our life reveals a character flaw we didn't realize we had. Too often we blame the person we're angry with. Or we blame the circumstances that caused us to react the way we did. No matter where we point the finger, we are refusing to point it at ourselves.

This trait has followed humanity throughout history. When Adam sinned in the Garden of Eden, he told God, "The woman you put here with me—she gave me some fruit from the tree, and I ate it" (Genesis 3:12). Adam was saying that his sin was either God's fault for putting Eve in the garden or Eve's fault for giving him the fruit. Sound familiar? If we are honest with ourselves, we'll admit that often we behave inappropriately. The question we must then ask ourselves is, *Am I willing to take responsibility for the way I behaved?* Sometimes it takes a circuit breaker to help us face that question.

I have been a jogger since 1969, running in a number of half-marathons and one marathon. A few years ago my knees began hurting. But I had such good times running with my friend David Davenport that it was worth the pain in my knees to jog with him a number of times each week. After the accident that left him a quadriplegic, I quit running. Almost overnight I gained close to twenty pounds.

There were many ways I could have rationalized the weight. I could have told myself that weight gain is a normal part of aging. I could have said this was a temporary weight gain that reflected my grief over my friend's accident. But the truth was that my years of running had masked my lack of control in the area of food.

Fortunately, my wife acted as a circuit breaker and helped me face that. She told me that if I was going to weigh as much as George Foreman, then I would have to fight him. Funny as that was, I couldn't laugh it off. I knew she was right. And I knew she had my best interests in mind by telling me. So I took responsibility for my excesses, muzzled my mouth, made some other changes in my lifestyle, and lost the weight.

We need circuit breakers to show us how we are hurting others. It's easy to be oblivious to the impact our behavior is having on those around us. We can unwittingly stomp on people's souls and leave them in the dust without feeling so much as a bump in the road. Often the bumps left behind are our own children.

My children have been a big help in showing me how hurtful I can sometimes be. A few years ago my grown daughter,

Stephanie, said on the telephone, "Dad, you always have to win." She was lovingly telling me that my *Driver* personality causes me to approach each conflict in a "win/lose" mindset. It took courage for her to tell me that, but I grew from the experience.

On another occasion I asked my then college-aged son, Michael, to attend a family event. I began to put pressure on him to show up. His response was, "Please don't 'guilt' me. If I come, it will be because I want to come, not because you made me feel guilty."

Surprised by his words, I asked, "Do I often 'guilt' you?"

"My whole life," he replied.

That was both painful and important for me to hear. I thanked him for telling me because he was helping me grow as a person and as a father.

We need circuit breakers to help us admit when we are wrong. God created us to be social people. We really *do* need one another. But we need each other for more than just companionship. We need each other for correction.

I sent an article about a fallen Christian leader to a friend, and he responded with this note: "There is a real shameful pattern here. God blesses, the man gets a big head, he becomes authoritarian with no outside voice talking to him, and then *crash!*"

A mark of maturity is our willingness to listen to outside voices, to people who point out something that may be a problem in our lives, even if they aren't terribly gracious about it. A Yiddish proverb says, "If ten people tell you you're drunk, lie down." If other people tell us we are rude, overbearing, or manipulative in our speech or behavior, we need to lie down— and listen.

We need circuit breakers to help us grow. A mark of spiritual maturity is the fruit of the Spirit in our lives. Paul identifies its characteristics as "love, joy, peace, patience, kindness, goodness, faithfulness, gentleness and self control" (Galatians 5:22-23). These are qualities the Holy Spirit uses to nourish others. He also uses these qualities in other people to nourish us.

I tend to take charge when a meeting begins to drift aimlessly, whether or not I've been given that right. On one occasion when I overstepped my bounds, a fellow pastor turned to me and gently asked, "Who's our leader here?"

It was an appropriate question, and I appreciated it, especially in light of his options. He could have remained quiet and said to himself, "Oh, that's just John. He's a take-charge kind of guy." Then I would have blindly continued to usurp someone else's authority. He could have embarrassed and demeaned me in front of the group by saying, "John, you are not in charge here." While that might have changed my behavior, it's also possible that because of my *Driver* personality style I would have made a bad situation worse by attacking him. Instead, he asked me a question that held me to a higher biblical standard: "You honor the leader you have." I was not the chosen leader, and he was willing to call me to account, but without meanness or insensitivity. It was a good question, gently asked, and it acted as a circuit breaker.

If we are going to grow and become more like Christ, we must invite others to ask those kinds of questions. We *don't* want to invite everyone we know to take his best shot at us. Such input from people who are immature or who don't have our best interests at heart can destroy us rather than build us up. But as we ask those who love us to tell us where we are falling short, the Holy Spirit will use them to produce the fruit of Christlike character.

PRINCIPLES FOR BEING A CIRCUIT BREAKER

Not only should we welcome circuit breakers into our own lives, we should be willing to be circuit breakers in the lives of others.

The letter to the Hebrews was written to a church that needed circuit breakers. It was full of both Jewish and Gentile converts. Think of the electricity that surged through the wires of that church! Some of the converts from Judaism had the attitude that they were still special people because Israel was still a special nation. They considered themselves a little more special than the Gentiles sitting behind them. Needless to say, the Gentiles weren't about to take a back pew. Picture Sunday morning. These were two groups of people with very diverse viewpoints trying to worship God under the same roof. How did they do it?

A letter to this church instructed them to put their heads together: "Let us consider how we may spur one another on toward love and good deeds. . . . Let us encourage one another" (Hebrews 10:24-25). The Greek word translated *consider* conveys a sense of precision and thoroughness. Back before we used calculators and computers, we would add columns of numbers manually. To do this, we had to pay close attention to each number and how it related to the numbers before and after it. That type of careful examination is what this word means. We aren't to reach conclusions about each other quickly or casually. Rather, we are to take the time to understand who other people are and how best to approach them about areas where they need to grow. Here are six principles we need to follow as we "spur one another on toward love and good deeds."

We need to look at other people with compassion. As difficult as it can be for us to see our own faults, it's all too easy to see the faults of those around us. Are we to ignore those faults? No. But we *are* to look at each other and consider how we can build each other up rather than how we can tear each other down.

Often we are critical of people who struggle in areas where we do not have problems. Although I lived in a fraternity house in college, I rarely drank, yet I wasn't critical of the guys who did. In fact, we used to go to the same parties. It's just that drinking never appealed to me. Because of that, I have no idea of the pressures alcoholics face as they try to avoid a drink. It would be easy for me to tell an alcoholic, "Just stop drinking," but such a statement would fail to acknowledge the depth of his or her struggle.

We also can be critical of situations where we don't have all the facts. We jump to conclusions. Perhaps a sudden weight gain is caused by some medication that we don't know a friend is taking. Perhaps someone's aggressiveness stems from an abusive relationship in her past and she's just trying to protect herself from being hurt again. Perhaps the short temper of a neighbor comes from some personal loss that we're unaware of.

Rather than criticize and find fault, we should figure out how to love and encourage these people. "Encourage one another and build each other up, just as in fact you are doing," instructed the apostle Paul (1 Thessalonians 5:11). To encourage one another means to "take counsel with another person." The idea of building each other up brings to mind the image of constructing a house. Each of us, as Paul said, must be careful how we build (1 Corinthians 3:10), discerning what is needed next in the lives of our friends so we will be able to give constructive counsel.

It is easy to look at other people in terms of how they are causing us problems, how they are weighing us down. We must remember that when we were rebelling against God, He was in the world reaching out to us. "He looked beyond our fault and saw our need," sang Dottie Rambo. Maybe that is where our lives need a revolution. Let's follow God's example and start looking beyond people's faults to their needs. Let's extend the same amount of grace and love to others that God has extended to us. If we will do that, the Holy Spirit will use us as circuit breakers in their lives.

We need to stand for truth. Although viewing others with compassion is important, it doesn't mean that we compromise biblical truth for the sake of friendship. Balancing truth and compassion is difficult, with most of us teetering in one direction or the other. But Jesus showed us how to maintain equilibrium in His encounter with the woman at the well (John 4). Here was a woman who had a tragic moral life. She had had five husbands and was now sharing bed and breakfast with a man who wasn't one of them. Rather than attacking her with that truth, Jesus asked her for a drink. This may seem insignificant to us, but it left the woman incredulous. "You are a Jew and I am a Samaritan woman. How can you ask me for a drink?" she said. John added the parenthetical explanation, "For Jews do not associate with Samaritans" (verse 9). In that one request for water, Jesus crossed cultural, religious, and gender barriers to establish a respectful relationship with a sinful woman.

By the time the conversation got around to the woman's moral life, Jesus had convinced the woman He truly cared for her. Not only did she listen to Him, she went to tell others about Him. The apostle John wrote, "Many of the Samaritans from that town believed in him because of the woman's testimony, 'He told me everything I ever did'" (verse 39).

Compare this with the "ministry" of the religious mind-police, as my friend Richard Davis calls them. They are the people who spend enormous amounts of time judging the behavior of others. They are always watching, always wagging a finger. They are terrible advertisements for Christ. They don't seem to enjoy life. And they don't seem concerned about building relationships that will allow them to have an eternal impact on others as Jesus did with the woman at the well. That should make all of us sad, and we would do Christianity a favor by loving them enough to tell them they are wrong.

We can confront people with their behavior without becoming rude and destructive ourselves. Jesus clearly did not approve of the lifestyle of the woman at the well, but He did not throw verbal stones at her or build barriers to their relationship. He saw what she could become if she began to worship God. He did not paint a bleak picture of her past. Instead, He painted a picture of her present life and then focused on what she could become. As we follow His pattern of being both compassionate and truthful, it's easier for others to see Jesus in our lives, making it easier for them to take a step closer and embrace Him for themselves.

We need to admit when our friends have weaknesses. It is often easier to be truthful about strangers than about our friends. But if we are going to be genuine friends, we must be willing to speak the truth in love, to help them see who they are and how they come across to others. If they are truly our friends, we shouldn't let them avoid areas in their lives where they fail to reflect the face of Christ.

The twenty-seventh chapter of Proverbs continually reminds us that true friendship involves honesty:

> Better is open rebuke than hidden love. (verse 5)
> Wounds from a friend can be trusted, but an enemy multiplies kisses. (verse 6)
> As iron sharpens iron, so one man sharpens another. (verse 17)

Too often we duck such confrontations. We "enable" our friends in their wrong behavior and attitudes in the name of mercy or tolerance. But mercy, tolerance, and enabling are distinct from each other.

- *Mercy* is the quality of seeing people's shortcomings and taking loving steps that give them the opportunity to better themselves. This is what God the Father did when He asked the Son to lay aside His deity, take on the form of a human being, and come to earth not only to die for our sins but to show us how to live.
- *Tolerance* is the quality of recognizing someone's shortcomings and bearing with him in the hope

that necessary changes will happen in the right time and in the right way. Many parents practice this when their teenage children go through periods of struggling with their identities and with life itself.

- *Enabling* is rationalizing or excusing wrong behavior in the life of a friend or family member. A friend of mine encountered such enabling one day when he met with the president of one organization and the vice-president of another. The president asked the vice-president why his president had not contacted him as he had promised three months earlier. The vice-president said, "Well, he has been extremely busy with an emergency in another city."

There may have been an emergency, but no one is so busy that in three months' time he can't write a note or make a phone call to communicate that he is up over his armpits in alligators. My friend asked the president in private how he felt about the explanation. His response was, "I felt as though he was lying to me and making excuses for his president's lack of good manners and competence."

When we make excuses for our friends, very few people are deceived, and we have done nothing to help our friends face up to their areas of weakness. If we are going to be circuit breakers, we must admit our friends' shortcomings instead of excusing them. And we must confront our friends about their shortcomings.

We need to speak in a way that will be heard. Anyone who has spent much time around young children knows how differently two children can respond to the same type of reprimand. Even in the same family, one child may be crushed by a stern look while another child bursts into laughter. These tendencies continue throughout our lives, and if we're going to be effective circuit breakers, we need to understand the sensitivity level of the people with whom we speak.

No one responds well to uncontrolled outbursts, icy stares, or manipulative whining. Before we try to be a circuit breaker in another person's life, we must ask ourselves, *Am I controlled by the Spirit of Christ right now?* If we can't speak with kindness and humility, or if we have sin in our lives that we haven't dealt with, then we have no business confronting anyone else.

If we have made sure that we are ready to express a concern to someone, then we must consider what approach will most effectively communicate our message. A sensitive person may be crushed by a direct statement, while a less sensitive person may miss the point entirely.

One of Susan's and my dearest friends is Katie Gerritsen. One day back in 1974, Katie worked up the courage to tell me, "John, I do not like to call your home to talk to Susan because I am afraid I will get you on the phone. You are so abrupt and curt that I always feel demeaned by you."

Her words had an undertone of wanting me to do better, to be a better person. She was not condemning or critical. She said what she needed to say in the context of love, friendship, and acceptance. The spirit she manifested that day allowed me to receive the truth of her words rather than react to them.

As effective as Katie's words to me were, they would not have had any effect on a denominational executive known to Harry Evans, former president of Trinity Seminary. This executive was the kind of person who wouldn't notice a two-by-four landing squarely on his head. So when he asked, "Evans, why does your board hate me?" Harry Evans responded, "I think it's because they think you're two-faced." Such bluntness would destroy many of us, but Harry Evans knew that this man wouldn't hear the message if it were delivered any less abruptly.

Jesus gave many examples of adjusting the tone of His message to His audience. The person who gently chided Martha with the words, "Martha, Martha, you are worried and upset about many things, but only one thing is needed" (Luke 10:41-42), is the same person who said to the religious leaders, "Now then, you Pharisees clean the outside of the cup and dish, but inside you are full of greed and wickedness" (Luke 11:39).

If we want to help others, we must speak the words they can understand, in the tone that is appropriate, with enough volume to get their attention.

We need to care enough to risk rejection. Being a circuit breaker isn't easy. While some people welcome input from others, many of us are resistant to correction. No matter how loving and compassionate we are, when we tell people about the inconsistencies in their lives, it is always possible that they will reject not only our words but *us.*

A friend of mine pastors a church in Minnesota that does not have air conditioning. In the summer, the humidity can be brutal. One sultry Sunday, he chose not to wear a suit coat. On that same Sunday, because a drama team was going to perform, the pulpit had been moved to the side. My friend was in the lobby, greeting people before the service, when a retired denominational executive approached him with a loud, disrespectful voice, berating him for not wearing a jacket and for moving the pulpit.

Later my friend called the man and said, "I do not care what you think of me, but I do care how you respect the office I hold and how you treat me in public. You, as a former pastor, should be exemplary in your behavior." In spite of the correction, which was respectfully given, the man would not apologize or admit he had done anything wrong. Instead he lashed out again.

My friend could have ignored the incident in the interest of keeping the peace. Instead, he held up a mirror to the retired executive. Because he did, he was rejected. Just because we try to make peace doesn't mean peace will be made. And sometimes the casualty of the peace process will be a broken relationship.

We need to be committed to helping our friends grow. In

Romans 15:14, Paul says, "I myself am convinced, my brothers, that you yourselves are full of goodness, complete in knowledge and competent to instruct one another." The word *instruct* can also be translated *admonish.* It means we are to put into a person's mind that which is needed to help him grow, something like planting a seed. We aren't simply interested in changing one specific behavior that bothers us; we want to see him grow and mature and become everything God created him to be.

A few years ago I was speaking at an African-American pastors' conference. A pastor from St. Louis spoke with me privately.

> You need to understand something as a white man
> about gangs in my neighborhood. They are deadly
> serious about brotherhood. They all have partners
> and when one is arrested and put in prison, while he
> is in prison his partner is to hold out half of every-
> thing he makes in crime so when his partner gets out
> of prison, he has something on which he can live
> until he gets back on his feet.

Now, if two people in a gang can have such a commitment to each other's *physical* well-being, how much more strongly should those of us who are in the family of Christ be committed to each other's *spiritual* well-being?

CHAPTER 10

LIVING THE GOLDEN RULE

It was a beautiful summer day in Portland, Oregon, as I stood in line to check my bags at the airport curb. At the front of the line was an expensively dressed man who had all the appearances of a prosperous, sophisticated traveler. When he left his bags and walked into the terminal without tipping, the skycap called after him in a rather loud voice, "Thank you."

The next man in line looked incredulous that such a distinguished-looking person had neglected to offer the customary tip. "Did he stiff you?" he asked.

"It happens," said the skycap with a shrug. As the skycap helped the second man with his baggage, they talked about how often people don't tip. The second passenger gave him a generous tip, and when he turned to go the skycap said, "As long as there are more of you than there are of him, this won't be a bad world to live in."

Over the past five years I've thought often about those two exchanges. The man who didn't leave a tip left the skycap feeling demeaned. The man who did left him feeling affirmed.

His actions demonstrate the Golden Rule: "In everything do to others what you would have them do to you" (Matthew 7:12). In many ways, that rule sums up the uncommon graces.

To help move that rule from a theoretical to a more practical place in your life, here are five tips—pardon the pun—that *I* would like to leave behind.

Be Committed to Following the Golden Rule

Many believers treat Christianity as an objective set of facts. They talk about "the faith." They argue points of doctrine. They defend the fortress of their beliefs. And they quote passages of Scripture to justify their diligence. But they forget that Jesus calls us to more than defending a statement of faith. The brother of our Lord raised that very issue when he said,

> Suppose a brother or sister is without clothes and daily food. If one of you says to him, "Go, I wish you well; keep warm and well fed," but does nothing about his physical needs, what good is it? . . . Show me your faith without deeds, and I will show you my faith by what I do. You believe that there is one God. Good! Even the demons believe that—and shudder. (James 2:15-19)

Faith reduced to a doctrinal statement—what good is that? It can't even distinguish us from the demons, James says. They believe there is a God. They even believe He's the God of the Bible. The contrast is that God *makes a difference* in our lives. Or He should, though it didn't seem that God made much of a difference in the life of a particular Christian professor.

He had assigned a paper to a class of doctoral students, and they waited anxiously to get them back. But the term ended, and they hadn't gotten them. The next term ended— still no papers. Eighteen months—nothing. The professor didn't get those papers back to his students for almost two years. He offered no explanation and gave no evaluation of the students' work. He simply assigned a grade.

Yet this same professor became furious when the school was a few days late paying him for a special project. He told the president that the school was failing to treat him in a Christ-like way. He wanted the institution to treat him with respect and pay him on time, but he felt he had the freedom to treat doctoral students with complete disregard. While he could see clearly the intellectual truth of the gospel, he was blind to how it should be lived out toward his students.

I wish I could say that this example is an isolated case. Unfortunately, it isn't. In fact, treating others as we would like to be treated has become so rare that people take special note of it. In his book *Wooden: A Lifetime of Observations and Reflections On and Off the Court,* former UCLA basketball coach John Wooden made this telling observation:

> I frequently received letters from custodians after we
> played an away game, telling me our basketball team
> had left the locker room neater and cleaner than any-
> one who had visited during the year. The locker
> rooms were clean when we departed because I asked
> the players to pick up after themselves. I believe this
> is just common courtesy. . . . Are managers and custo-
> dians the players' servants?[1]

Whether we apply it to locker rooms or to board rooms, the Golden Rule can transform our lives and touch the lives of those around us. I thought of that when I received this letter from John Taylor, a fraternity brother of mine who is the principal at a public junior high school in Salem, Oregon:

> It seems so amazing to me that for all the twenty-
> seven years I have been in education, we have skirted
> the Golden Rule. Countless hours have been spent in
> designing plans, schemes, and techniques for dealing
> with misbehavior. For so long it had seemed like a
> losing battle.

For the past two years, I have been working with
staff, parents, and students on an idea that I have
truly held dear since I was in elementary school
myself. I feel like we have allowed ourselves to talk
about respect in a very open way. Kids do respond to
this idea. It is so simple. We even say—in a public
school, yet—"Do unto others. . . ."

My view is that we have all been yearning for
this Golden Rule/respect idea. You can see with the
way the kids respond that its time is here . . . not that
it ever left.

In our school we even talk about respect at the
start of each assembly. We have had much positive
feedback from parents, guest speakers, and per-
formers. Of course, there is much left to be done.
However, we are encouraged by the results we are
seeing and the seeming desire on the part of our
school community to have the greater degree of
peace that mutual respect can bring to our lives.

John captured the essence of the Golden Rule in the phrase
"mutual respect." The apostle Paul captured it in other words:
"Each of you should look not only to your own interests, but
also to the interests of others" (Philippians 2:4).

Acknowledge Where We Fall Short of the Golden Rule

If we are going to follow the Golden Rule, we must understand
where we fall short. Perhaps one of the best ways to start eval-
uating ourselves is to take a minute to think about how we like
to be treated ourselves. I was speaking at a conference on this
subject and asked the audience how they like to be treated.
Here are some of their answers:

- Give me the freedom to be myself.
- Treat me with honesty.
- Be helpful to me when I am in need.
- Give it to me straight.
- Help me improve and grow.
- Treat me with courtesy.
- Treat me with respect.
- Treat me with patience.
- Encourage me.
- Listen to me.
- Take the time to understand me.
- Love me.
- Trust me.
- Don't be selfish with me.
- Be kind.
- Be sensitive if I am in pain.
- Don't use me.
- Don't always insist you are right.
- Don't insist you didn't say what others claim you did.

Most of us would agree with this list, but next comes the hard part. We must ask ourselves some tough questions: *Was I treating my child with respect tonight when I lost my temper? Did I listen to the person at the meeting who disagreed with me, or was I too busy formulating my response? When was the last time I admitted to someone that I was wrong?*

It is hard to examine ourselves, harder still to admit our shortcomings. But it is only as we are willing to face our areas of weakness that our ability to live out the Golden Rule increases.

LISTEN WHEN OTHERS TELL US THAT WE ARE FALLING SHORT

A successful pastor who's been in the ministry for over thirty years will never forget one couple. In his own words, here's why.

One time, Janet (not her real name) was looking for an assistant pastor who was in my office. She came in, never looked at me or acknowledged me, and conducted her business with my assistant. In *my* office. Another time she was upset about some decision the elders and staff had made, and she verbally assailed the wife of the youth pastor in a hallway between services—even though the wife of the pastor had no idea what the woman was talking about.

The pastor went on to describe an incident in which the husband of this woman had been unhappy with some decisions the pastor had made. Instead of calling for an appointment—and this man was a high-level executive who should have understood proper procedure—he wrote his complaints on the back of a pledge envelope.

The man hadn't asked for a response from the pastor, but my friend made a lunch appointment with him anyway. He listened to the man's complaints and suggested, "Let me repeat the essence of what you have said so you can confirm that I have heard you correctly." Having determined that he understood his parishioner's complaints, the pastor said, "Now if, after thinking and praying about what you presented, I decide not to change our direction, can I count on your support?"

The man responded, "No. Why would I do that?"

This husband and wife call themselves Christians, yet their lives show a pattern of disregard for authority, neglect for common courtesy, and a refusal to tolerate any difference of opinion. Why do they seem so willing to demean others and treat them so rudely? Why do they violate the Golden Rule so often and so easily? Like most of us, they may intend to treat others well but are blind to how boorishly they behave. They desperately need someone who loves them to tell them the truth about their behavior and how far removed it is from the Golden Rule.

It seems we all have a built-in self-defense mechanism that

keeps us from initially admitting that we might be wrong, that our behavior may be less than what God desires. Here is just one example. About twelve people wanted an organization to go in one direction, while one wanted it to go in another. Because of the difference of opinion, the one person resigned from the organization. This is perfectly acceptable. The problem is this man's refusal to admit that he said certain things in meetings with the other twelve people. They can cite the place, the time, the chair he sat in, the words he used, but he simply responds by saying, "I did not say that."

To practice the Golden Rule means that we open ourselves to people and the possibility that they could be right. Instead of building our defensive skills to protect ourselves, thereby cutting ourselves off from intimacy and community, we need to be continually opening ourselves to others, to their ways of thinking, and to the possibility that they may have the correct view.

This is not always easy, especially if we have lived our lives making certain we always get our way. We cannot realize how much we violate the Golden Rule until we listen to those who tell us how we treat other people.

BE REALISTIC ABOUT OTHERS LIVING BY THE GOLDEN RULE

A friend of mine, whom I'll call Jim, is a missionary in Latin America. He was home in the United States when a businessman repeatedly asked him to apply for the job of assistant pastor at the businessman's church. The businessman lives in a big house and drives a luxury car. He kept talking about the "great opportunity" in his church. When Jim asked about the salary, he got a long answer that gave no specifics but was peppered with reassurances that this job was a great opportunity.

Jim later discovered from another source that the assistant pastor's salary was about 60 percent of his missionary salary, which was already quite low. The businessman was asking Jim to move his family from Latin America to an upper-middle-class community in the United States where the average price of a home is seven times the salary being offered.

In the businessman's rush to convince a good person to fill a vacancy, he neglected to consider the issues that would be important to Jim. The man didn't live by the Golden Rule. And if Jim believed that every Christian who crossed his path was living it, he might have found himself in a situation where he couldn't provide for his family.

Jim's situation is an extreme example, but it's surprising how many of us assume whenever we deal with Christians that they will automatically follow the Golden Rule. We must recognize that we're all sinners. We all have moments when we are selfish rather than considerate—even as believers.

Jesus was quick to acknowledge our fallen nature when He gave two instructions to His disciples: "I am sending you out like sheep among wolves. Therefore be as shrewd as snakes and as innocent as doves" (Matthew 10:16). Jesus doesn't want us to find ourselves in bad situations that could have been avoided. He wants us to be shrewd, to recognize that people who claim to be God's children can prey on us as certainly as wolves prey on sheep. On the other hand, He doesn't want us to use the failings of others as an excuse for not being Christ-like in return. Are we to confront people who wrong us? Yes. But never with predatory instincts, and never going for the jugular. Shrewd, yes. Innocent, yes. Ruthless, never.

Be Dependent on God

As we grow in our understanding of the Golden Rule, it will change how we live. See how it changed the way this salesman lived. He was ready to close a deal and collect a large commission for what amounted to very little work on his part when all of a sudden the Golden Rule popped into his head. He realized that the person to whom he was selling did not need his product, and at that moment he was faced with a decision. He could do for himself, or he could do unto others. He struggled but chose the latter. He treated the person the way he would have wanted to have been treated. He told the person the truth. As a result, the sale didn't go through. Neither did his commission.

We follow the Golden Rule not because there's something in it for us. We follow the Golden Rule because it is the right thing to do, regardless of the lost sales, the lost commissions, or the lost jobs. Living the Golden Rule is where our faith puts on its walking shoes. With one foot we trust. With the other we obey. And that's how we walk with God. Obeying His commands. Trusting His care. Step by step, that is how He wants us to go through life. Just as the writer of Proverbs says, "Trust in the LORD with all your heart and lean not on your own understanding; in all your ways acknowledge him, and he will make your paths straight" (3:5-6).

The more we focus on living out the Golden Rule, the more we can depend on God to guide us and care for us. When God brings about that change in our lives, our perspective of others will change. That is when we will be able to accept those who are different from us and appreciate them for the unique individuals God created them to be.

I'm thinking of a very unique individual. Here's his story. Early in his childhood, this boy developed a zany personality, learning to hang from trees while imitating an ape. I told you he was unique. He learned to suck in a great amount of air and expel it in loud, lion-type roars. *Very* unique. One time as a high-school student, he hid in the bushes and made his lion sounds, which were so convincing the neighbors got scared and called the police. His friends howled with laughter. Over the years, though, the laughter turned to ridicule.

He was beginning to think that there wasn't a place for him—outside the zoo—until he found a place at a parachurch youth ministry. The director of the ministry saw that his antics could build team spirit and inject a little needed humor. Eventually the director became a pastor, and their paths went in different directions. Recently, the pastor got a letter from the young man which read: "You were the first person I had ever worked with who really made me feel of great value and worth—that my crazy personality was needed, even wanted."

Value me the way you would like to be valued. Need me the way you would like to be needed. Want me the way you would like to be wanted. That was the cry of the boy's heart— a cry the Golden Rule was meant to answer.

Who wouldn't respond to being answered like that?

Depending on God also opens us to being more compassionate toward others. I was reminded of this recently when I was speaking at a conference where I had become reacquainted with a man I hadn't seen in twenty years. Back when we were in seminary, he lost his right arm in an industrial accident. I asked him how the accident had affected him during the intervening years. He said that he asked God to use his tragedy to make him more sensitive and compassionate to hurting people. "I had to give my right arm to learn it, but I believe I have learned it." He told me that it's too easy to see only people's scars and not recognize the pain behind them. This is true whether the scars cover a place where an arm has been amputated or some other place, some unseen place of unspeakable pain.

Unspeakable pain, in one case, cowered within the soul of a young girl. When she was thirteen, her father's best friend raped her. She told her father, but he didn't believe her. When her parents divorced, her mother remarried. Then the young woman's stepfather raped her. Again and again, her soul was scarred with the message that she was worthless. She escaped her miserable home life through the back alley of drug abuse.

Eventually she ended up in a crack house where she turned tricks in exchange for whatever drugs she could get. She was so lonely and so desperate that she remembers praying as she was going off into another crack-induced stupor, "God, please let my dog be here when I come to." Her dog was the only friend she had.

When she woke up, the dog was there. It was a small and seemingly insignificant answer to prayer. But it proved to her that God loved her. It was God who brought her to my friend's church. There, for only the second time in her life, she encountered a man who cared about her as a person, not as a woman whose body could be taken, used, and thrown away. My friend and the people of his church are being used by God to transform her life.

Does she have behavior they don't agree with? Of course. Habits they don't appreciate? Certainly. But instead of condemning her, they are showering her with love. Why? Because that is what God did for us. "While we were still sinners, Christ died for us" (Romans 5:8). He took the first step. His love was not based on our actions. His love, in fact, preceded our actions. Can we do any differently? "As the Father has loved me, so have I loved you," Jesus told His disciples. "Now remain in my love. If you obey my commands, you will remain in my love" (John 15:9-10).

His love. That's what it all boils down to. Receiving it, then giving it away. Always giving it away.

But we're living in a time when nobody's giving away much of anything, least of all love. We're living in a time when the rule is "look out for number one," and there's nothing very golden about *that*. In just such a time, God has called us to remain in His love. To show that love by treating others as we would want to be treated ourselves. To fill the world with uncommon graces.

It's time.

It's time these uncommon graces became common. Starting

with us. With you, the reader. And with me, the writer. It's time they became common in us.

If they are not common in us, God help the church.

And if they are not common in the church, God help the world.

EPILOGUE

THIS ENTIRE ISSUE OF MAKING A DIFFERENCE CAN SEEM DAUNTNG, I will admit. Some days it does seem easier to contemplate retiring to the golf course, the fishing boat, or the hills, and letting the world frantically rush by. But Jesus said He came to serve, not to be served. His followers must be servants, too.

Where do we start? With the first tree. Let me explain what I mean by that by introducing you to Frosty Westering.

You cannot be a football fan in the Pacific Northwest without knowing the name Frosty Westering, the head football coach at Pacific Lutheran University. Twice his teams have been national champions, and twice they were second in the nation. The secret of Coach Westering's success is to maximize the talents God has given and not to try to be anyone else. He illustrates this secret in his book *Make the Big Time Where You Are!*

> A group of middle-aged businessmen asked me years ago if I would help them develop a personal fitness program. They all had physical examinations and we had our first meeting together in sweats, shoes, the whole works. I shared with them the key concept of competing against yourself: ME vs. ME—learning to challenge your best self and not others. After going over all the other areas of warm-up, stretching and progressive workouts, I asked them to write down on a 3x5 card how far they believed they could jog at a

constant pace before they would feel the stress and
then stop. I put flags around the track at each 110
yards, to help them estimate their distance. As we did
this, Ralph, a short heavyset man, got up and started
to leave. While the others were getting ready for their
warm-up, I caught up to him and asked what was
wrong. "Frosty," he said, "I'm embarrassed—all
these other men are going out there and will jog so
much further than I can. I'm a joke—and I'm just not
going to do it." "Ralph," I said, "I have shared with
you how important it is to compete against yourself,
to challenge yourself and not compare yourself to
others. When you learn to do that, you will start to
enjoy the challenge and competition of becoming
your best self." "Frosty, that sounds good, but that
isn't how it works—everyone compares you to
others and in my case it's a no win." I looked Ralph
in the eyes and said, "How far do you think you can
jog before you feel stress?" He didn't answer. "Can
you go one lap?" He shook his head. "How about a
half lap?" "I couldn't do that," he said. "How about a
straight-away?" Before he could respond, I looked
and saw a big tree about fifty yards away. I said,
"Ralph, how about the big tree?" He looked at the
tree and replied, "I can make the tree." "Let's go," I
shouted. So he and I jogged to the tree. As soon as we
got there, I exclaimed, "Ralph, we made it—you're a
one-tree man." He gave me a puzzled look, but his
eyes lit up when I said, "This is where you start, one
tree." His look now turned into a smile and he said,
"Frosty, you're right, this is where I start—I'm a one-
tree man."

Six weeks later Ralph was a 43-tree man.

He jogged near a wooded area and counted trees
instead of laps. Forty-two trees was a little over a

mile. His progress was exciting, and he loved the new challenge of ME vs. ME. He even placed a tiny tree in his office every time he reached a new one in his workout. Believe me, after a while *he had a jungle in there, and he loved it.*[1]

Just as Ralph did, we start with one tree, one uncommon grace that we would like to make common in our life. Pick one, any one, and start there. Maybe it's mercy. Maybe it's attentiveness. Or maybe it's kindness. It doesn't matter *where* you start. It matters only *that* you start. Here's a story about one man and how he started.

Humorist Andy Rooney of *60 Minutes* tells of climbing into a cab on the busy, dog-eat-dog, survival-of-the-fittest streets of New York City. He was expecting cold silence or a gruff hello. Instead, the cabby turned around and smiled. And that was only the beginning. During the entire trip, the cabby was cordial and talkative. This guy wasn't your normal New York cabby, Rooney concluded. He asked the man why he was so polite and courteous toward customers.

"I'm out to change New York," the cabby explained.

"But you're just one guy," Rooney replied.

"I know, but I figure if I show kindness to you, you'll show it to the next person you meet, and they'll pass it on to someone else. It'll be like a big expanding ripple, spreading out through the whole city."

Perhaps that cabby was naive about his ability to change a city of millions. But perhaps he was on to something. And perhaps you and I can get in on it, too.

Our world *can* be changed. That's why God sent His Son, slipping into our world through a watery birth in the stable of a small town. He wanted to make some universe-sized waves that would roll out into the world and spill out into eternity.

All it takes is to manifest *Uncommon Graces* in a hostile world.

NOTES

Introduction

1. Martin J. Smith, "Common Courtesies Forgotten in the Rude, Crude U.S.," *The Arizona Republic* (31 October 1994), p. C-8.
2. Smith, p. C-8.
3. Smith, p. C-8.
4. Smith, p. C-8.
5. Smith, p. C-8.

Chapter 1

1. Kevin Diaz and Pat Phiefer, "Police Chief Laux to Retire," *Minneapolis StarTribune* (21 October 1998, vol. 13, no. 204), p. 1A.
2. Martin J. Smith, "Common Courtesies Forgotten in the Rude, Crude U.S.," *The Orange County Register* quoted in *The Arizona Republic* (31 October 1994), p. C-8.
3. Dr. Dennis Baker, personal letter used by permission.

Chapter 2

1. John Wesley, *Sermons on Several Occasions* (London: The Epworth Press, 1944). The sermons were part of forty-four discourses published in four volumes in 1746, 1748, 1750, and 1760.
2. Jim Wooten, "The Conciliator," *New York Times Magazine* (29 January 1995, vol. 164, no. 48.948), p. 33.
3. Ken Sylvester, "How to Transform a Competitive Environment into a Collaborative Environment" (Organization Strategy Institute, Issaquah, Wash., 1992, unpublished material).

Chapter 3

1. Dr. Paul Tournier, *Secrets* (Richmond: John Knox Press, 1968) p. 15.

Chapter 4

1. Tony Kennedy, "No Matter How You Slice It," *Minneapolis StarTribune* (11 October 1994, vol. 13, no. 194), p. 1A.
2. Richard Hoffer, "Fistful of Dollars," *Sports Illustrated* (January 1990, Vol. 72, no. 2), p. 94
3. John Danforth, *The Resurrection: The Confirmation of Clarence Thomas* (New York, NY: Beacon Books/Viking Press, 1994), p. 68.
4. The following letter is used by permission.

Sometimes we live in a world of assumptions, unfortunate as it may be. We assume things are going along just fine because we are not aware that a problem exists. Our dental practice is based on relationships not just teeth. We constantly deal with people's fears, apprehensions and dental problems. Because of these problems people often-times choose to ignore them hoping they will go away or not happen again so they don't have to address them. Sometimes they are just too "Minnesota nice" to say any-thing. Unfortunately for us if these problems are not addressed, they perpetrate not only affecting the original person but rather patients and ultimately our practice.

Because our relationship was one that went beyond teeth, you were willing to risk that relationship. I believe that your faith told you that if you addressed the problem at hand it could be dealt with in everybody's best interest—a win-win situation. Your uncommon grace helped me to see what I didn't see. It helped us to have more open, candid relationships within our office and with our patients. It helped us to have a better dental practice.

Since then we have encouraged people to be more candidly blunt in a respectful manner when there is a problem that needs to be addressed. We have sat down with each specialist we refer to and explained how we expect our patients to be cared for. Our staff is informed—from day one—that it is their responsibility to address a prob-lem when they first become aware of it. We encourage our patients to do the same. This past year we sent out a patient survey requesting feedback (good and bad) about our practice so we could improve how we care for our patients.

You helped us with your uncommon grace. Hopefully, we have passed it on. I believe that ultimately that is our purpose in life—to help each other. I also told your pub-lisher that it would be okay to use my name. This was a real event and if a name helps to add credibility to the story, use it. Anonymity may detract from reality.

Since our conversation the person we discussed has not changed. We have not referred a patient to that office since then.

Again, thank you for your "gentle response."

Sincerely,

Michael John Harrison, D.D.S.

5. David Goetz and Marshall Shelley, "Standing in the Crossfire: An Interview with Bill Hybels," *Leadership Journal* (Winter 1993, vol. 14), pp. 20-21.

Chapter 5

1. Chuck Hutchcraft, "A Revealing, If Sometimes Soft Look at Abrasive Work Places," *Chicago Tribune* (January, 1997), p. 3.

Chapter 6

1. Charles Allen, *Love Is Patient, Love Is Kind* (Nashville, Tenn.: Abingdon Press, 1989), p. 21.
2. Philip Yancey, "Christian McCarthyism," *Christianity Today* (18 July 1994, vol. 38, no. 8), p. 72.

Chapter 7

1. John Haggai, *How to Win Over Worry* (Eugene: Harvest House, 1987).
2. George Will, *This Week With David Brinkley*, 12 February 1995.
3. Steve Wulf, "The Paint Master," *Sports Illustrated* (24 August 1992, vol. 77, no. 8), p. 62.
4. George Vecsey, "Too Early for a Gooden Movie?" (*New York Times*, 16 August 1996, Vol. CXLIV, Number 50,531).

5. Anthony G. Winterowd, "Life's Difficult Issues: Avoiding Mean-Spirited Legalism" (M. Div. diss. Talbot Seminary, 1996), p. 6.

6. Philip Yancey, "Christian McCarthyism," *Christianity Today* (18 July 1994, vol. 38, no. 8), p. 72.

7. Peter McCleery, "Dialogue on Golf: Hale Irwin," *Golf Digest* (1994 October, vol. 45, no. 10), p. 106.

8. Jill Lieber, "Yankee Pitcher Seizes 'Second Chance at Life,'" *USA Today* (27 February 1996, vol. 14, no. 58), p. C1.

9. Sheila Walsh, *Honestly* (Grand Rapids, Mich.: Zondervan, 1996), pp. 56-57.

Chapter 8

1. *USA Today*, (August, 1996), p. 4A.

2. Mary Pipher, Ph.D., *Reviving Ophelia: Saving the Lives of Adolescent Girls* (New York, NY: Ballantine, 1994).

3. C.S. Lewis, *The Weight of Glory and Other Addresses* (Grand Rapids, Mich.: Eerdmans, 1965), p. 15.

Chapter 9

1. Scott Peck, *People of the Lie* (New York, Simon & Schuster, 1983) p. 74.

2. David Merrill, *Style Awareness Simplified: An Overview* (Personal Predictions and Research, Inc., Denver, 1976).

Chapter 10

1. John Wooden, *Wooden: A Lifetime of Observations and Reflections On and Off the Court* (Lincolnwood, Ill.: Contemporary Books, 1997), p. 76.

Epilogue

1. Frosty Westering, *Make the Big Time Where You Are!* (Tacoma, Wash.: Big Five Productions, 1990), p. 37.

Author

JOHN VAWTER spent ten years on the staff of Campus Crusade for Christ both in England and as Northwest Area Director. He pastored at Wayzata Evangelical Free Church in the suburbs of Minneapolis for fourteen years. Before becoming the pastor of Bethany Community Church (which has an attendance of two thousand on Sunday morning), he was president of Phoenix Seminary. He has taught doctoral courses in six different seminaries and spoken in fourteen different countries. He has been married to Susan for thirty-one years. Their two adult children are Stephanie and Michael.